AF521958

The Book of Revelations:
a Commentary

Translated from the French
Original title : APPROCHE DE LA CITÉ CÉLESTE
COMMENTAIRES DE L'APOCALYPSE

Omraam Mikhaël Aïvanhov

The Book of Revelations: *a Commentary*

Collection Izvor
No. 230

EDITIONS  **PROSVETA**

Prosveta S.A. – B.P. 12 – 83601 Fréjus Cedex (France)

ISBN 2-85566-491-8

édition originale : ISBN 2-85566-476-4

Readers will better understand certain aspects of the lectures published in the present volume if they bear in mind that the Master Omraam Mikhaël Aïvanhov's Teaching was exclusively oral and that the editors have made every effort to respect the flavour and style of each lecture.

The Master's Teaching is more than a body of doctrines: it is an organic whole, and his way of presenting it was to approach it from countless different points of view. By repeating certain aspects in a wide variety of contexts he constantly reveals a new dimension of the whole and, at the same time, throws new light on the individual aspects and on their vital links with each other.

TABLE OF CONTENTS

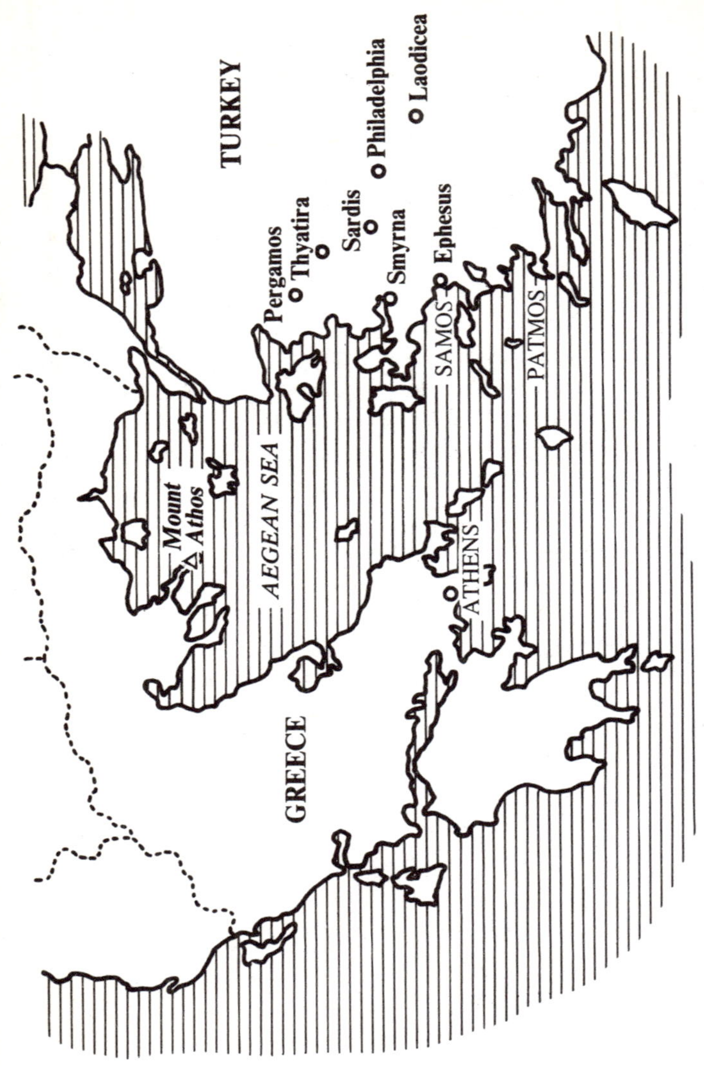

Map of Greece and Asia Minor
showing principal places mentioned in the text

Chapter One

THE ISLAND OF PATMOS

I want to take you with me today as I go back to visit a place that won my heart and the hearts of all those who were with me when we first visited it together. Come with me; let me take you a long way from here and let us visit this blessed place, the Island of Patmos.

Although Patmos is a Greek island it is much closer to Turkey than to Greece. The only access is by boat and the trip from Athens takes nearly thirteen hours. Patmos is a tiny island, a mere dot on the map, but its spiritual importance makes it immense and it is this immensity that we had set out to explore. Our visit was a pilgrimage, you see; a pilgrimage to the place in which St John had lived and in which he wrote his Gospel and the Book of Revelations.

As one approaches the island, the first thing that strikes one is the immaculate whiteness of the houses. A whiteness that is all the more dazzling set against the blueness of sky and sea. Some of the island's little villages are built by the sea; others, like Khora, are up in the hills and it is there, in Khora, that we find the monastery of St John the Evangelist and the cave of the Apocalypse. In the course of the centuries, many buildings have grown up round the cave in which St John lived and it is these buildings that constitute the monastery. They include the Basilica of St John the Divine[1], built on the ruins of a temple dedicated to Artemis, a chapel dedicated to St Christodoulos, the founder of the 12th century monastery, and many other churches and chapels as well as the monks' cells, a refectory, a library and so on. The whole complex, which can be seen from every point on the island, is surrounded by the fortifications built in the 17th century, when it was necessary to defend the place against the frequent incursions of pirates. It is an impressive sight.

The only entrance to the monastery is at the top of a short flight of steps cut out of the rock. Corridors, inner courtyards and flower gardens flanked by cells and chapels, lead from the entrance to another flight of about thirty steps, also cut out of the rock. At the bottom of these steps are still more chapels and, finally, we come to the chapel of St Anne which gives directly on to the cave of the Apocalypse. This little chapel was the first to be built and Christodoulos dedicated it to St Anne in honour of the mother of Mary (Jesus' mother) and of Anne, the mother of Alexius I Comnenos, the Byzantine

[1] Divine meaning theologian, from the Greek name for St John: John the Theologue.

Emperor of the period[2].

The cave of the Apocalypse itself is neither very big (it can contain only a few people at a time) nor very high (six or seven feet). We were shown a hollow in the rock which is traditionally believed to have served as a pillow on which St John rested his head, and above this hollow is a cross which the Saint is said to have engraved in the rock. There is also another hollow on which he is said to have leaned for support when he stood up, for he was already very old.

One part of the rock is very straight and smooth with a kind of ledge and we were told that this was where his disciple Prokhoros wrote the Gospel to St John's dictation. In the arched roof of the cave is a triple opening which is said to have been made by the thunderbolt that fell when the voice of the Apocalypse was heard; this triple crack in the rock is considered to be a symbol of the Trinity. The cave also contains several sacred objects and icons with lamps burning in front of them and on the walls are various inscriptions in Greek: 'In the beginning was the Word'; 'It was here, at Patmos, that these things happened', and 'This place of dread'.

The priest who showed us round pointed out innumerable treasures everywhere: magnificently illuminated manuscripts, relics, icons and all kinds

[2] It was the Emperor Alexius I Comnenos who gave Christodoulos the Island of Patmos.

of sacred objects, and when he related many details of St John's life - based on the testimony of some of the Saint's disciples here, at Patmos - he was in such an extraordinary state of inspiration and rapture, he hardly knew what was happening to him. He was quite radiant.

I visited the cave twice to meditate and be in communion with the spirit of St John, and was much struck by the quite extraordinary quality of the silence. After two thousand years and in spite of the countless visitors that have been in and out, nothing has been able to wipe out the fluidic traces left by St John the Evangelist on those rocks. I could sense so many things in this cave, for it is a truly sacred, a truly pure, divine place. I hope that you will all have the opportunity to visit it one day.

In the first chapter of Revelations, St John himself tells us why he was at Patmos. 'I, John, both your brother and companion in tribulation, and in the kingdom and patience of Jesus Christ, was on the island that is called Patmos for the word of God and for the testimony of Jesus Christ.'

During the persecution of Christians in the reign of the Roman Emperor Domitian, St John was arrested in Ephesus and, accompanied by his disciple Prokhoros, sent in chains to the island of Patmos. Tradition has it that while they were at sea a violent storm arose and the sailors were hard put to it to keep the ship on course because of the huge waves. Suddenly, to the horror of the passengers, a young soldier fell overboard and the boy's father was in such despair that he tried to throw himself over the side, wanting to join his son in death; the other passengers had great difficulty in holding him back. In the midst of all this emotion only St John remained imperturbable; in fact, he seemed almost to be pleased about the accident. They asked him, 'Doesn't the boy's death mean anything to you? Can't you do something to help us?' 'Why don't you ask your own gods?' St John replied; 'Perhaps they would save him.' But they replied, 'We have been imploring them for hours already in vain'. So St John began to pray and, within a few minutes, the boy appeared on the surface of the water and was rescued, unharmed by his ordeal. Everybody was astounded. They surrounded St John, thanking him and asking him to forgive them for putting him in chains. Then they released him from his bonds and treated him with great respect.

When St John disembarked at Patmos he was taken to live with the family of a man called Myron and, while living in his house, he drove out the evil spirits that had taken possession of Myron's children and did so much good to all around him that his renown spread throughout the island and more and more people came to consult him. Gradually, he began to talk to them about Jesus, to tell them who he was and what he, himself, had witnessed as his disciple, and many of those who heard him were converted. In this way, Myron's house became the first meeting place for the Christians of Patmos.

Yes, but there was also a sanctuary on Patmos dedicated to Apollo and the growing influence of St John enraged the priests of Apollo, for their temple was soon abandoned by the population. At the head of these priests was a dangerous black magician called Kynops, and the priests decided that Kynops should get rid of St John by sending a very powerful demon to attack him. But St John wrestled with the demon and defeated him. Then Kynops sent a second, more powerful demon, accompanied by a third, whose task was to report to him on the outcome of the struggle and, when this second demon was defeated in the same way, Kynops decided to confront St John himself.

Accordingly, he set out and found St John preaching to a crowd of people. Interrupting his discourse, Kynops began to question a boy in the crowd: 'Where is your father?' he asked. 'He's dead', replied the boy; 'He was lost at sea.' Turning to a man standing by, Kynops asked, 'And you, there: where is your son?' 'He's dead' replied the man; 'He committed suicide by throwing himself overboard.' Others said the same thing; they all had members of their family who had drowned accidentally or on purpose and, turning to St John, Kynops challenged him to bring all those drowned men up from the bottom of the sea. To this St John replied that his mission was not to raise the dead but to preach the Gospel of Jesus. Kynops, delighted to have the chance to show his superiority, then performed some magic rites and brought out of the sea a semblance of each of those who had drowned. The people, taken in by these sorcerer's tricks believed in Kynops's power again and, spurred on by him, turned and attacked St John who fell to the ground, grievously injured; then they all went home, very satisfied with the day's work, convinced that St John was dead. During the night, however, the disciple Prokhoros came to where St John was lying and heard his voice saying, 'Prokhoros, go and tell Myron that I am still alive and that I'll be coming back to the house. Everything's going to be all right.' When Myron heard the good news he was astonished and delighted.

It was not long before the war with Kynops began all over again and went on for a long time. Then, one day, a crowd of people dragged St John to the beach where Kynops was again performing his magic rites in order to prove, once and for all, that he was more powerful than St John. St John prayed and, when Kynops dived into the sea, saying that he was going to bring back the semblances of the dead men, he disappeared. For three days many people waited on the beach hoping to see him coming out of the sea, but in vain: Kynops never came up again but, by his words and attitude St John finally persuaded them to accept the teaching of Christ and to go home quietly. Today, people will point out a rock in the sea which has three parts and will tell you that they are the petrified head, trunk and members of the sorcerer Kynops.

Not many years after these events the Emperor Domitian was assassinated and his successor, the Emperor Nerva, proved to be more tolerant towards the Christians. Under his rule the persecutions came to an end and St John was allowed to leave Patmos and return to Ephesus. Of course, by this time, St John had enlightened, helped and healed so many of the inhabitants of the island that they had become deeply attached to him and did not want him to leave. They begged and implored him to stay, but he told them, 'I must go; there are other brothers and sisters who are waiting to hear the Good News' and, although they continued to implore him, he was adamant. At last, when they realized that they could not prevent him from going, they asked him to write something for them before he went; something that would be a reminder of the Good News he had brought them. This St John agreed to do and, after several days of prayer and fasting, he began to dictate his Gospel to Prokhoros: 'In the beginning was the Word ...' followed by the Book of Revelations. When this was done, the inhabitants of Patmos understood that he had given them all they needed and they let him leave.

Our guide at Patmos told us that, at the end, when St John felt that death was near, he asked two or three of his disciples to dig a big hole in the ground. Then he got into the hole and told them to fill it up with soil as far as his chest and to come back the next day. When they came back St John was still alive. He told them, 'Bury me up to my shoulders and come back tomorrow'. The next day he was still alive and he asked them to add a little more soil. When they came back the following day he was no longer there. Of course, this must be just a legend. There are a great many more or less legendary stories about St John which are said to have been handed down in oral or written form by his disciples and I was told that some of them can be seen in certain libraries in Greece. I would be very interested to learn some of the details they talk about.

Throughout the centuries, ever since the earliest days of the Church, there has always been a tradition at Patmos that takes its inspiration from the teaching of St John. It was because of this tradition that, in the 18th century, a school was founded not far from the monastery. This school, known as Patmias, has enriched Christianity by producing numbers of churchmen, theologians and thinkers, some of whom were very remarkable people.

Patmos is such a magnificent place that I would have liked the Greek Brotherhood to have a piece of land there so that they could go and stay on the island from time to time. What exceptional conditions they would have had for prayer and meditation and a brotherly life together! And how much they would have enjoyed growing melons and all kinds of fruit trees! In fact, the taxi driver who drove us to the monastery owned several plots of land on the island; I noticed one of them in particular on the top of a hill which he said he was willing to sell us. It had a wonderful view of the sunrise and you could see a number of other islands in the distance, as well as the monastery and the harbour with all its little houses. Patmos is not so very far from Athens but, unfortunately, it takes a long time to get there and the journey cannot be made by air. The only way to get there is by boat: thirteen hours there and thirteen hours back again, and if the sea is choppy - as it was when we were there - it is quite an expedition.

The surprising thing is that, before this journey, I had always feared to travel by boat because I suffered from seasickness. But this time it was just the opposite: I found it most exhilarating to be tossed about by the waves; I enjoyed it enormously! Yes, you may well laugh! Anyway, to satisfy this new-found need to be tossed up and down, we hired a small motor launch and sailed about for a couple of days and visited Mount Athos. What a magnificent visit that was too! There are twenty or more monasteries scattered about the mountain and we visited at least half of them. The Bulgarian name for Mount Athos is Sveta Gora which means 'holy forest'. We went to various Bulgarian, Yugoslav and Russian monasteries and saw some extraordinary icons. How beautiful they are! Of course, we took lots of photos and films and the monks were so hospitable and friendly, they did not want us to leave.

They kept pressing Turkish delight, preserves, coffee and even rakia on us. If we had accepted all that they offered we would never have found our way back to our boat!

But to get back to Patmos. One of the things that most enchanted me while we were there was the beauty of the place; there is something very simple about it, for there is very little vegetation. It is principally the atmosphere that is so extraordinary, as though the spirit of St John had penetrated deep into the ground and into its inhabitants. Even now, two thousand years later, Patmos is still a truly exceptional place; in spite of all the people who have visited it, in spite of the tourist trade which usually causes devastation wherever it appears and which destroys the simple, natural mentality of warm-hearted, hospitable people by bringing with it some of the worst aspects of modern life. In fact, the people of Patmos really astonished me: the glow in their faces and the simple dignity of their ways made me feel that this was a very special place. I have never met such people anywhere, people capable of manifesting so much love, kindness, sincerity, generosity and brotherliness. Yes, their mentality is so brotherly and so mystical, religious and profound! One has the impression that no one in Patmos is bad or dishonest. We saw almost all the inhabitants, from those who came to meet us at the boat and carried our suitcases, to the monks and bishops, and they were all so charming, so warmly welcoming - there are no words to express it! I assure you, it would be well worth your while to go there just to meet those people. Their faces expressed such peace, happiness and light. Yes, a light emanated from them; one could feel and see their aura.

One day, after I had spent some time meditating and burning incense in my hotel room, asking the Invisible World for the answers to some questions, my travelling companions and I went out for a walk in the hills. On the way, we saw an old woman standing beside the path ahead of us. She was simply, even poorly, dressed but she had a wonderful face and she was just standing there, as though waiting for us. When we came closer, she stepped up to me and, kissing my hand with great respect, said a few words in Greek. When her words were translated for me I realized that they were the answer to the questions I had been asking. Heaven had spoken to me through that old woman. You cannot imagine how happy that made me! Yes, because her words were prophetic; she had given me Heaven's answer to my questions. It is very easy for Heaven to give us answers through a bird, a dog or a horse - and, of course, even through another human being. The only problem is that we are not always capable of deciphering or understanding those answers, but they are always available; Heaven never leaves us without an answer. And the answer I got from Heaven that day was a great joy to me. After this episode we went on and visited some of the other marvellous spots on the island.

Truly, there is something very special about Patmos. Many of the people we talked to had a way of expressing themselves that I had never heard in any other town or country in the world. What they said was so wise and profound and their language had such an extraordinarily mystical, spiritual quality to it. Nor have I ever met priests and monks who were so kind and so radiant. Many of them came to see me and we had long conversations together. And what a joy it was to meet all those friendly faces in the streets and to see the respect, trust and love with which they looked at us. This is truly a land in which people are happy; a land of innocence and purity. God bless it!

Chapter Two

INTRODUCTION TO THE BOOK OF REVELATIONS

When Christianity first appeared it did not suddenly burst upon the world from nowhere. It was the fruit of several traditions and, in particular, of the Judaic tradition represented by the Cabbalah. Jesus himself was familiar with the Cabbalah and it is essential for anyone who wants really to understand the Old and New Testaments to have a working knowledge of that vast science. Unfortunately, the Church has been content, for centuries, to hand on only a few scraps, a few superficial notions of this science to the faithful. Is it any wonder, then, that Christians today think that Christianity is poor and inadequate and are more and more inclined to go and look for spiritual nourishment in the teachings of the Middle and Far East? Who is to blame for this state of affairs? The clergy should be ashamed to have been incapable of showing the faithful the great wealth and depth of Christianity and of its philosophy and symbolism. They have been content with too many empty exhortations which taught people nothing and this is the result: all those who want something more leave the Church.

For centuries, Christians have been told that the only thing that was essential was to have faith. When they asked questions about their religion they were told that it was a mystery and that they should not try to understand: they only had to believe and they would be saved. But that is false: it is not enough to believe. Religion is not only a question of faith. Every religion possesses a body of science and, if the faithful are not allowed to nourish their minds, souls and spirits with this science, they end by losing their faith, because they have the impression that they are being asked to believe something absurd.

I know that a great many people will have difficulty in accepting the idea that Jesus was familiar with the Cabbalah; but that is the truth. The Cabbalah was an integral part of the Judaic tradition in which he was brought up and it was he who revealed it to St John. This is why we find so many cabbalistic elements in the Gospel and the Apocalypse[1] of St John.

In all spiritual traditions there is an exoteric teaching that is given to all the faithful and an esoteric teaching that is reserved for the small spiritual elite capable of understanding it. The exoteric aspect of the Christian religion is represented by the Church of Peter: the Church that has imposed itself by force, that has never hesitated

[1] The Apocalypse is the usual French name for the Book of Revelations.

to massacre and burn all those who opposed it or who, without really opposing it, seemed to be unwilling to accept its rules. The esoteric teaching of Christianity, on the other hand, is represented by the Church of St John: the Church that has always carried on its work in secret, that has never persecuted or massacred anyone, but that has, on the contrary, always been a victim of the intolerance of the Church of Peter.

Jesus gave St John a teaching that he did not give to the other disciples, therefore; and the others, when they realized this, were a little jealous. But let's leave that for the time being. The important thing is that the Church of St John is the guardian of the quintessence of Jesus' doctrine and is always ready to teach those who manifest the desire to study the secrets of creation and the truths that concern the invisible world and the spiritual development of human beings. Revelations is the book of the Church of John, but, in order to interpret the numbers, symbols and images it contains, one has to know something about the Cabbalah as well as about astrology, alchemy, magic and even the cards of the Tarot - which are not playing cards, as many people imagine, but an abstract of Initiatic Science.

This is why most priests and pastors avoid any attempt to interpret Revelations for that would oblige them to accept all these other sciences and, consequently, to change certain aspects of their religion. Yes, they neglect this book because it proves that the Scriptures cannot be interpreted without the help of Initiatic Science. They prefer to imply that St John, who was very old when he wrote it, said such improbable things because he had allowed himself to be influenced by the rabbis or even because he was not in his right mind. Yes, instead of studying and learning to decipher and understand St John's symbols they prefer to ignore the whole thing on the pretext that he was senile!

Some of you may say, 'Yes, but it is true that Revelations is terribly obscure and difficult to interpret!' That is true for those who do not possess the key to it, but for those who possess the key it is extremely clear. To be sure, the images, symbols and numbers are not always in the order in which one might expect to find them: some of those which are at the end of the book relate to passages at the beginning or in the middle. It is as though a pack of cards had been thrown haphazardly onto a table. But he who possesses the true science can pick up those cards, put them back in order and read them. Once one knows the hidden meaning of the numbers and symbols, all the elements that seem to be entirely unrelated fall into place and shed light on each other and the result is an extraordinarily logical whole.

I have read a great many interpretations of the Apocalypse and although some of them, of course, are true as far as they go, I have found that none of them has ever really gone all the way and plumbed its depths. Why? There are several reasons for this but the main one is that, instead of concentrating on its essential message: a description of the elements and processes that are common to our own inner life and the life of the cosmos, their authors have been more concerned with trying to identify the historical characters, countries and events depicted. As a result, a lot of nonsense has been written about the four Horsemen, the Beast with seven heads and ten horns, the Woman crowned with stars, the great Harlot, the New Jerusalem, etc.

I too have interpreted some passages from the Apocalypse for you and I could continue to do so but there are so many other things that must be dealt with first. What possible use can the Apocalypse be to you if you have never worked to acquire the true foundations of the spiritual life? For it is not enough to understand all these symbols intellectually, you have to be able to make them come alive within you. As long as this preliminary work of purification, self-control and inner elevation has not been done you will never be able to enter the marvellous realm of the Apocalypse.

Chapter Three

MELCHIZEDEK AND INITIATION INTO THE MYSTERY OF THE TWO PRINCIPLES

'I, John, both your brother and companion in tribulation, and in the kingdom and patience of Jesus Christ, was on the island that is called Patmos for the word of God and for the testimony of Jesus Christ. I was in the Spirit on the Lord's Day, and I heard behind me a loud voice, as of a trumpet, saying ... "What you see, write in a book and send it to the seven churches which are in Asia: to Ephesus, to Smyrna, to Pergamos, to Thyatira, to Sardis, to Philadelphia and to Laodicea."

Then I turned to see the voice that spoke with me. And having turned I saw seven gold lampstands, and in the midst of the seven lampstands One like the Son of Man, clothed with a garment down to the feet and girded about the chest with a golden band. His head and His hair were white like wool, as white as snow, and his eyes like a flame of fire; His feet were like fine brass, as if refined in a furnace, and His voice as the sound of many waters; He had in His right hand seven stars, out of His mouth went a sharp two-edged sword, and His countenance was like the sun shining in its strength.

And when I saw Him, I fell at His feet as dead. But He laid His right hand on me, saying to me, "Do not be afraid; I am the First and the Last. I am He who lives, and was dead, and behold, I am alive for evermore".'

Revelations 1, 9-18

For the last two thousand years, theologians and exegetists have been trying to decide on the identity of this mysterious being described by St John at the beginning of his Revelations. All kinds of answers have been suggested. Some say that it was God Himself but that is not possible, for no man has ever seen God. Others say that it was Jesus but I cannot accept that either, for St John knew Jesus so well that he would have recognized him at once and exclaimed, 'Master, how glad I am to see you!' But he didn't say anything of the kind. In fact, not only did he fail to recognize that extraordinary being from whose mouth issued a sword and whose eyes were like flames, but he fell to the ground as though struck by lightning. Some scholars have suggested that it was an Archangel or perhaps Tsaphkiel, the chief of the Angelic order of Thrones. No, the Being who appeared to St John was Melchizedek.

From time immemorial, one great Initiatic centre has existed on earth which is over and above all others. All the lesser centres are simply branches of this unique centre whose light has never ceased to shine throughout the centuries, and to guarantee the continuity of this bright flame there had to be a Being who possessed all powers and all knowledge, a Being who could be God's representative on earth, a Being who would never die. For the earth needs the perpetual presence of God's representative. And this Being actually exists; he is mentioned in the Bible and in all the spiritual traditions of the world, although under different names; it is not possible to doubt his existence.

In the Hebrew tradition he is known as Melchizedek, king of Salem. The name Melchizedek means 'king of justice' (from the Hebrew *melek*, meaning 'king', and *tsedek*, meaning 'justice'). And Salem, the name of the city of which he was king, comes from the word *shalom*, meaning 'peace'. (We find the same root in the Hebrew name of Jerusalem: *Ieruschalaïm*, and of Solomon: *Schlomo*). Melchizedek, therefore, is the king of justice and peace, but that is practically all we know; he is a very mysterious being. Only the great Initiates know anything about him and he is mentioned only rarely in the Bible.

In Genesis, Moses gives us his account of the meeting between Abraham and Melchizedek. `And the king of Sodom went out to meet him at the Valley of Shaveh (that is, the King's Valley), after his return from the defeat of Chedorlaomer and the kings who were with him. Then Melchizedek, king of Salem brought out bread and wine; he was the priest of God Most High. And he blessed him and said: "Blessed be Abram of God Most High, Possessor of heaven and earth; and blessed be God Most High, who has delivered your enemies into your hand." And Abram gave him a tithe of all.'[1]

Naturally, this passage should not be taken quite literally. Melchizedek, the greatest of all high Initiates did not go out to meet Abraham because he had conquered a few hundred or a few thousand enemies on the field of battle. Abraham's victory over the seven sinister kings of Edom represents his victory over the seven deadly sins and Melchizedek offered him the bread and wine as a reward for that victory. Of course, many people think that this was not much of a reward but that is because they don't understand its symbolic importance. In fact, the bread and wine represent the whole of Initiatic Science, the Science that is based on the two cosmic principles perpetually at work in every region of the universe: the masculine principle (symbolized by the bread) and the feminine principle (symbolized by the wine). This was the reward that Melchizedek brought to Abraham. And Abraham bowed down before him and, as a sign of his gratitude, gave him the tithe of all his possessions, that is to say, he dedicated to him all the wealth of his heart and soul and spirit.

Melchizedek manifests himself to all Initiates who succeed in reaching the summit. It is he, the

[1] Genesis 14, 17-20.

Master, who seeks out his disciple and not, as many people imagine, the disciple who chooses his Master. A Master knows who is capable of being his disciple whereas a disciple - who does not always have a very clear idea of what he is looking for - may decide to follow a Master and then abandon him for another and then another. A lot of people think that they are the disciples of a Master who, in fact, does not recognize them as such.

It is the superior, therefore, who takes the initiative and goes out to meet the inferior. Melchizedek went out to meet Abraham to give him his blessing and when Abraham, who knew that he was the inferior, gave him the tithe of all he possessed, Melchizedek initiated him into other mysteries. Abraham adored Chadai-el-Hai, God Almighty, the Deity that corresponds to the region of the Sephirah Yesod, and Melchizedek, who was the priest of the Most High, revealed God to Abraham under that name (El-Elion in Hebrew)[2]. The Most High is the name that the Cabbalah attributes to the highest manifestation of the Deity, that which corresponds to Kether, the first Sephirah.

The only other passage in the Bible that speaks

[2] Compare with the opening verse of Psalm 91, 'He who dwells in the secret place (or shelter) of the Most High shall abide (or rest) in the shadow of the Almighty': *Ioschev* (he who dwells) *beseter* (in the shelter) *Elion* (of the Most High) *betzel* (in the shadow) *Chadai* (of the Almighty) *itlonan* (rests).

of Melchizedek at any length is in St Paul's Epistle to the Hebrews. St Paul writes: 'For this Melchizedek, king of Salem, priest of the Most High God, who met Abraham returning from the slaughter of the kings and blessed him, to whom also Abraham gave a tenth part of all, first being translated "king of righteousness," and then also king of Salem, meaning "king of peace", without father, without mother, without genealogy, having neither beginning of days nor end of life, but made like the Son of God, remains a priest continually. Now consider how great this man was, to whom even the patriarch Abraham gave a tenth of the spoils.'[3]

You will ask, 'But if he had no father or mother, how was he created?' A being who is God's representative on earth is all-powerful in respect to matter. By the power of his spirit, which is the spirit of God Himself, he can form or disintegrate a body at will. Matter obeys him. This is why Melchizedek is called the priest of the Most High. The true spiritual meaning of the term priest is 'sacrificer', he who possesses the secret of the transmutation of matter.[4] For sacrifice, in fact, is simply that: a transmutation, a transformation by which matter becomes purer and more luminous. To be the priest of the Most High is to exercise the most sublime

[3] Hebrews 7, 1-4.

[4] For a fuller discussion of the meaning of sacrifice, see *Complete Works*, vol. 17, chap. 5.

function in the whole universe, for it is he who offers to God the purest quintessence of matter.

Of all God's representatives it is Melchizedek who has the most important role to play on earth. All decisions and instructions concerning the destiny of mankind come from him. All the high Initiates received their instruction from him: Hermes Trismegistus was an aspect of Melchizedek and Orpheus, Moses, Pythagoras, Plato, Buddha and Zoroaster - all the greatest Initiates were taught by him: even Jesus. It was Melchizedek who sent the three Magi, as representatives of his kingdom, to bow down before Jesus, because Jesus was the incarnation of the Christ-principle, of the Word made flesh. But Melchizedek, representative of the living God, who has neither beginning nor end, has another role to play.

Jesus, therefore, received instruction from Melchizedek. St Paul states this very clearly when he explains that Jesus belonged to the order of Melchizedek. 'So also Christ did not glorify himself to become High Priest, but it was He (God) who said to him: "You are My Son, Today I have begotten you." As he also says in another place: "You are a priest forever according to the order of Melchizedek".' And in another passage, St Paul says, 'This hope we have as an anchor of the soul, both sure and steadfast, and which enters the Presence behind the veil, where the forerunner has entered for us, even Jesus, having become High

Priest forever according to the order of Melchizedek'.[5] St Paul had been the pupil of the cabbalist Gamaliel; it was he who had taught St Paul about Melchizedek and the order to which Jesus belonged.

As I have said, Melchizedek revealed God to Abraham as El-Elion, the Most High God, and it is interesting to note that El-Elion has the same numerical value as Immanuel, which was the name of Jesus. St Matthew's Gospel tells us that Joseph was visited by an Angel who told him that a son would be born to Mary. Quoting the words of the Prophet Isaiah, the Angel said, 'Behold, a virgin shall conceive and bear a Son, and they shall call His name Immanuel'. And in St Luke's Gospel we read that the Archangel Gabriel appeared to Mary and announced, 'And behold, you will conceive in your womb and bring forth a Son, and shall call his name Jesus. He will be great, and will be called the Son of the Most High.'

Of course, I know that some Christians will protest in horror and tell me that it is blasphemous to say that Jesus belonged to the order of Melchizedek, because that means that Melchizedek was of a higher rank than Jesus. Yes, that is true. But it is not I who say that; it is St Paul. If Christians are determined to be shocked by the idea, that is their problem. In any case, they are fated to be shocked again and again

[5] Hebrews 5, 5-6 and 6, 19-20.

until they make up their minds to accept the truth.

Jesus incarnated on earth because he had received the mission to give human beings an example and show them what a son of man could do. Whereas Melchizedek's mission is to remain hidden, to avoid manifesting himself to human beings. His work is different from that of Jesus and this is why he has never taken flesh in the womb of a woman as Jesus did. In reality, therefore, it is only in their mission that they are different; Jesus possesses the same nature, the same elevated rank and the same light as Melchizedek. If this were not so, why would St Paul have associated Jesus and Melchizedek?

Jesus, then, was of the order of Melchizedek and the most striking proof of this filiation is the rite instituted by Jesus at the Last Supper: during this last meal with his disciples, Jesus renewed the offering of bread and wine that Melchizedek had made to Abraham. 'As they were eating, Jesus took bread … and gave it to the disciples and said, "Take, eat; this is my body." Then he took the cup … and gave it to them, saying, "Drink from it, all of you. For this is my blood. Do this in remembrance of me … Whoever eats my flesh and drinks my blood has eternal life".'[6]

This sacred rite is re-enacted every day at Mass when the priest consecrates the bread and wine so that they may become the body and blood of Christ.

[6] Matthew 26, 26-28; Luke 22, 19-20; John 6, 56

If you want to understand the meaning of these words you must know that bread and wine, the product of wheat and grapes, are symbols of the masculine and feminine principles which are present in almost all Initiations. Bread and wine can become the body and blood of Christ only because they are solar symbols. On the cosmic plane, the body and blood of Christ are the light and warmth of the sun which creates life; on the spiritual plane, the body and blood of Christ are wisdom and love. What Jesus was saying, therefore, was, 'If you eat my body - wisdom - and drink my blood - love - you will have eternal life'.

Holy Communion is one of the essential rites of the Christian religion and yet, in the two thousand years in which Christians have been receiving Communion, one might well wonder how many of them have obtained eternal life. Yes, for it is not enough to take the bread and wine or the host consecrated by a priest. Every man and every woman must themselves be a priest, a 'sacrificer'; every man and woman must come before all the cells of his body with an offering of bread and wine, that is to say: with the gift of love and wisdom.

The sacrament of the Eucharist by which Christians partake of the body and blood of Christ and, thereby, of divine life, is an extremely powerful magic rite. It is to this sacrament that Christianity owes its strength and the fact that it has endured throughout the centuries. So why should we not expand our understanding of such sacred matters?

During the eighteen years of Jesus's life which is not mentioned in the Gospels, he was studying and working in the Kingdom of Melchizedek. It was there that he received Initiation before returning to Palestine, at the age of about thirty, in order to accomplish his mission. But he also put his disciples in touch with this Kingdom of Melchizedek. There is a tradition common to all religions that this Kingdom exists in some inaccessible region known as the 'land of the immortals' or 'land of the living'. It is to this land that the Psalmist refers when he sings, 'I will walk before the Lord in the land of the living'.[7] It is also the land known as Agharta or as the Kingdom of Prester John. In reality it is the Kingdom of Melchizedek, but only a few Initiates who are in touch with Melchizedek actually have firsthand knowledge of it. When Jesus said 'Seek first the kingdom of God and His righteousness, and all these things shall be added to you', he was referring to this Kingdom of Melchizedek, king of righteousness.

No Initiate can reach the summit unless he has been enrolled in the School of Melchizedek. It is he who confers the highest degrees of Initiation; it is he who is the one true Master of all the greatest Masters - and only of the greatest. From the beginning he has been the incarnate presence of the Cosmic Christ on earth. He watches over the evolution of mankind,

[7] Psalm 116, 9.

guiding it according to God's plan and, when human beings go too far in transgressing the divine laws, it is he who intervenes and restores order. As the four elements, earth, water, air and fire are at his service, he has all powers.

It was Jesus who asked Melchizedek to manifest himself to his disciple John. Official Christianity never mentions these facts but they are recorded in the archives of Initiatic Science and anyone who is capable of going to look for them will find them there.

The being whom St John saw in his vision, therefore, and who declared, 'I am Alpha and Omega the beginning and the end' was none other than Melchizedek. His name changes according to the cycles of the ages, because it is magic. In Greek mythology he is known as Minos, king of Crete, son of Zeus, judge and lawgiver; in India he is known as Manu. When I was in India I asked some sages whether their tradition spoke of a being who never dies and I was told that it did and that his name was Markandeya. So, as you see, this being is known by different names in different religions and cultures, but it is always the same being.

Melchizedek, who reigns over the destiny of the world, is an aspect of Christ, the Cosmic Principle. This is what St Paul means when he says that he was 'made like the Son of God'.[8] There must always be, somewhere on earth, a divine fire whose flames are

[8] Hebrews 7, 3.

never extinguished and this is precisely the task of Melchizedek: to keep this fire alive. He is this fire and all those who are ready to do so can light their own flame from his.

II

So, as we have already seen, the being seen by St John and whom he describes at the beginning of Revelations was Melchizedek. The seven golden lampstands that surrounded him mean that he possessed all knowledge; the seven stars in his right hand mean that he possessed all power, and the sword issuing from his mouth means that he possessed the power of the Divine Word: by the power of the Word he sets in motion, guides and controls events. The two edges of the flaming sword in his mouth show that he had power over both good and evil: he sets free the spirits of light and binds the spirits of darkness.

Jesus, who was, in the words of St Paul, 'Sacrificer of the Most High according to the order of Melchizedek', also possessed the power of the Divine Word. It was by the power of the Word - the Logos - that he drove out demons, healed the sick and raised the dead, and he transmitted this power to his disciples, telling them, 'Whatever you bind on earth will be bound in Heaven, and whatever you loose on earth will be loosed in heaven.'

On several occasions in Revelations, Melchizedek says, 'I am the Alpha and the Omega, the Beginning and the End, the First and the Last'. Revelations was, of course, written in Greek and the letters *alpha* and *omega* are the first and last letters of the Greek alphabet. In Hebrew, which is the language of the Cabbalah and which was also the language of Jesus and St John, the first and last letters of the alphabet are *aleph* and *tav*. But why this mention of letters of the alphabet? What makes a letter so significant that a being as exalted as Melchizedek should say, 'I am the Alpha and the Omega'?

In French or English, when we speak of Mr. X or Mrs Y, we mean anyone and everyone or, at any rate, someone who is not worth identifying. But we cannot interpret Melchizedek's declaration that he is 'the Alpha and the Omega' - or 'Aleph and Tav' - unless we take into account the symbolic function of the letters of the alphabet in the Judaic tradition. For a cabbalist, letters represent infinitely more than they mean to us, infinitely more than the letters we use every day when we write. Also, the two letters *aleph* and *tav* must not be seen in isolation: between the first and last letter of the alphabet are all the others. The beginning cannot be separated from the end any more than your head can be separated from your feet. An alphabet is a body, a living whole formed of a number of elements - the letters - and the order in which they follow each other is not a question of chance.

For a cabbalist, the twenty-two letters of the Hebrew alphabet are the analogical representation of the twenty-two elements used by God in the creation of the world. The *Sepher Yetzirah* or Book of Creation, attributed to Abraham, says that, in the beginning, God summoned the letters and gave each of them a particular mission in the creation of the world. The three Mother letters, *aleph* א, *mem* מ and *shin* ש, were charged with the creation, respectively, of air, water and fire. The seven double letters, *beth* ב, *ghimel* ג, *daleth* ד, *kaph* כ, *pe* פ, *resh* ר and *tav* ת, created the seven planets. The twelve simple letters, *he* ה, *vau* ו, *zayin* ז, *cheth* ח, *teth* ט, *yod* י, *lamed* ל, *nun* נ, *samekh* ס, *ayin* ע, *tsade* צ and *kof* ק, created the twelve constellations of the Zodiac. Thus these twenty-two letters, which embrace the whole of creation, represent the elements, forces, virtues, qualities, spirits and powers which were combined to create the universe. By means of these living letters, God formed words and sentences. And He continues to form words and sentences. This was how the world was created and continues to be created.

When Initiates study the letters of the Hebrew alphabet, therefore, they do so in order to read and understand the living language of nature. 'I am the Alpha and the Omega' means 'I am the Word, the twenty-two elements by means of which the world was created'. And, here again, we see the connection between the Apocalypse, which is divided into twenty-two chapters (the same number as the letters of the Hebrew alphabet) and St John's Gospel which opens with the words, 'In the beginning was the Word, and the Word was with God, and the Word was God ...All things were made through Him, and without Him nothing was made that was made.' These two books, the Gospel and the Revelations of St John, both of which are so essential to Christianity, are dominated by the theme of the Logos, the creative Word.

The trouble is that most human beings use words, the faculty of speech, in such prosaic ways that they can no longer understand this creative role. The form of creation they know above all others is that which produces a child: the act of procreation in which a man and woman unite to bring a child into the world. But there is a close analogy between these two forms of creation. How is speech produced? By the mouth which has a tongue and two lips: the tongue represents the masculine principle and the lips the feminine principle, and when they act together they produce speech, the child. If you simply open your mouth you cannot produce words, only sounds. In order to produce articulate speech, the lips and tongue must work together; in other words, the masculine and feminine principles must be united.

When it is a question of creating a child, since the two principles exist separately, the woman on the one side and the man on the other, the creative power of each is incomplete; they have to come together in order to create - and this is where so many complications begin: novels, plays and films are full of the adventures (comic or tragic) of men and women who want to come together in this way. In God, however, the two creative principles are never separated; this is why God creates without ceasing. A complete being possesses both principles.

Now, don't misunderstand me: I am not saying that human beings should possess the two principles on the physical plane; that would be ridiculous. Even though a theory exists according to which the first human beings were hermaphrodites, we have to accept that, in present conditions, the masculine and feminine principles are separate. It is on the spiritual plane that human beings must achieve the unification of the two principles - the principles of love and wisdom - for it is only in this way that they will dwell in truth and be truly strong.

What is a magus? A magus is someone who, first and foremost, possesses knowledge but who also possesses love, and it is this love that enables him to vivify his knowledge. When he speaks, his Word is saturated with that light and warmth, with that wisdom and love, and it is this that makes it powerful. It is this that enables him to make his influence felt in the whole of creation, throughout the visible and invisible worlds; it is this that gives him the power to set in motion men, Angels and Archangels, spirits and the elements. You must understand that everything is part of a whole and that there is an analogy, an absolute correspondence between man and the cosmos and between all the different kingdoms of nature. The sun speaks. Yes, the sun speaks and its Word is life; the sun speaks and its Word is the light that falls on the earth, on us, on plants and animals and all beings.

And now, let's say that the tongue is the father and the lips the mother and that their speech is the child. This means that what the father gives the mother is the creative Word, the Word that animates and gives life. Just as the sun fertilizes the earth and man fertilizes woman, the Divine Word fertilizes souls and hearts. The one who speaks is the father, the one who listens becomes the mother and the sentiments, emotions, thoughts and actions that are born are the children.

By telling you these things I am gradually reconstructing for you part of the teaching of the two principles that Melchizedek gave to Abraham. Perhaps you can now understand why the androgyne, that is to say, a being who possesses both masculine and feminine principles in himself, is the symbol of a high Initiate. In order to bring the Divine Child, the Divine Word to birth within himself, he needs to be both father and mother, man and woman. An Initiate is a being fulfilled. If you want to make progress in the spiritual life you have to know how the same rules apply in all regions, on all planes and in all worlds.

Chapter Four

LETTERS TO THE CHURCH IN EPHESUS AND SMYRNA

'To the Angel of the Church of Ephesus write, "These things says he who holds the seven stars in his right hand, who walks in the midst of the seven golden lampstands: I know your works, your labour, your patience, and that you cannot bear those who are evil. And you have tested those who say they are apostles and are not, and have found them liars; and you have persevered and have patience, and have laboured for my name's sake and have not become weary. Nevertheless I have this against you that you have left your first love. Remember therefore from where you have fallen; repent and do the first works, or else I will come to you quickly and remove your lampstand from its place - unless you repent. But this you have, that you hate the deeds of the Nicolaitans, which I also hate.

He who has an ear, let him hear what the Spirit says to the Churches. To him who overcomes I will give to eat from the tree of life, which is in the midst of the Paradise of God".

And to the Angel of the Church in Smyrna write, "These things says the First and the Last, who was dead, and came to life: I know your works, tribulation, and poverty (but you are rich); and I know the blasphemy of those who say they are Jews and are not, but are a synagogue of Satan. Do not fear any of those things which you are about to suffer. Indeed, the Devil is about to throw some of you into prison, that you may be tested, and you will have tribulation ten days. Be faithful unto death, and I will give you the crown of life.

He who has an ear, let him hear what the Spirit says to the Churches. He who overcomes shall not be hurt by the second death".'

Revelations 2, 1-11

These messages to the Church in Ephesus and Smyrna - like those that follow to the other Churches - start by formulating a judgement followed by some advice and conclude with a promise of reward for those who overcome. To the Church in Ephesus it is promised that he who overcomes will be rewarded with the fruit of the Tree of Life, whereas the Church in Smyrna is told that he who overcomes 'shall not be hurt by the second death'. What does this mean: to 'eat of the Tree of Life' and 'to be hurt by the second death'? In order to understand these images, we must first examine the question of man's two natures, the higher and lower natures about which I have often spoken to you[1].

[1] See *Collection Izvor*, No. 213, 'Man's Two Natures, Human and Divine' and *Complete Works*, vol. 11, 'The Key to the Problems of Existence'.

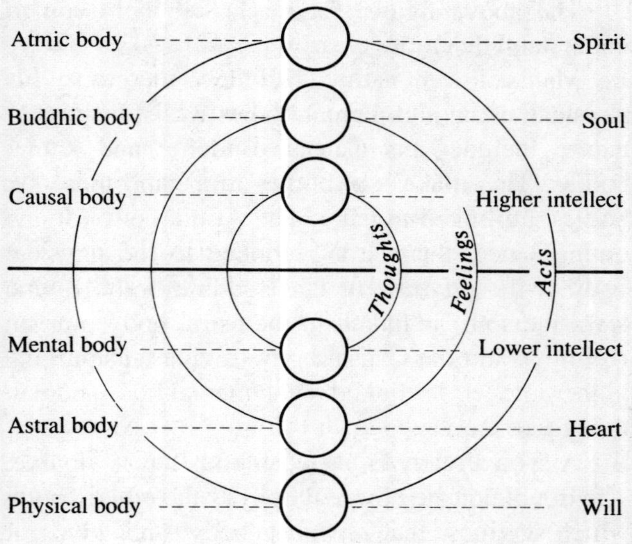

Figure 1

Man is characterized essentially by the threefold manifestation of thought, feeling and action, which corresponds to his three faculties of mind, heart and will. And, depending on whether he allows his higher or his lower nature to express themselves, the thoughts, feelings and actions he produces are ordinary or even negative and destructive or, on the contrary, luminous, noble and constructive.

The above figure (Figure 1) will help you to understand this more clearly.

Man's lower nature includes, therefore, his physical, astral and mental bodies whilst his higher nature includes his Causal, Buddhic and Atmic bodies. This makes six bodies in all and these six bodies are linked in pairs. The Atmic body (divine omnipotence, the spirit) is linked to the physical body (will and action); the Buddhic body (divine love, the soul) is linked to the astral body (human feelings), and the Causal body (divine wisdom, the higher intellect) is linked to the mental body (human thoughts).

As you already know, each body has its double. The double of the physical body is the etheric body which vivifies the physical body and gives it sensitivity, and the situation is identical for all the other bodies. The figure will be more complete, therefore, if we indicate each body and its double by means of two interlocked circles and add the corresponding signs of the Zodiac and planets. See Figure 2[2].

[2] For a fuller explanation of this figure, see *Complete Works*, vol. 2, chap. 2.

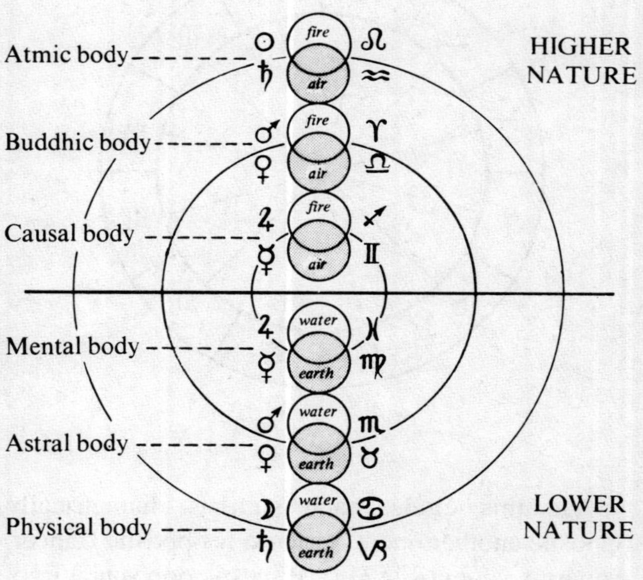
Atmic body
Buddhic body
Causal body
Mental body
Astral body
Physical body
fire
air
fire
air
fire
air
water
earth
water
earth
water
earth
HIGHER
NATURE
LOWER
NATURE

Figure 2

And now let us study the circle of the Zodiac.

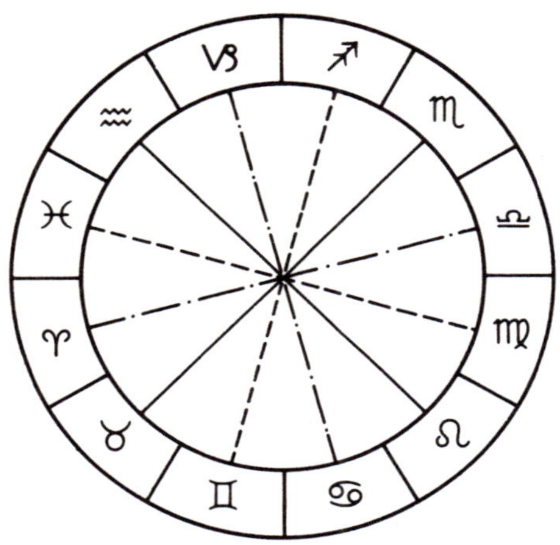

Figure 3

On this circle, each sign is diametrically opposite another one: Capricorn is opposite Cancer, Aquarius is opposite Leo, Pisces is opposite Virgo, etc., and each of these relations means something.

In the previous figure, we saw that the astral body is ruled by Mars and Venus; and Mars incites to violence and destruction while Venus unleashes sensual passion. But the astral body is linked to the Buddhic body and the Buddhic body is ruled by the higher aspect of the same planets. Each planet, as you know, has two opposite aspects; Mars, for instance, which can be the expression of anger and aggression, can also manifest itself as courage, dynamism, the spirit of chivalry that takes up arms in defence of the weak. And Venus does not only manifest itself as selfish, sensual love but also as spiritual love. Each planet, therefore, has two houses, one in the lower half of the figure and the other in the upper half.

On the lower level, Venus and Mars are in the signs of Taurus and Scorpio; on the upper level they are in Libra and Aries, and in the circle of the Zodiac, Aries is opposite Libra and Taurus is opposite Scorpio.

So now let's have a closer look at these two sets of polar opposites.

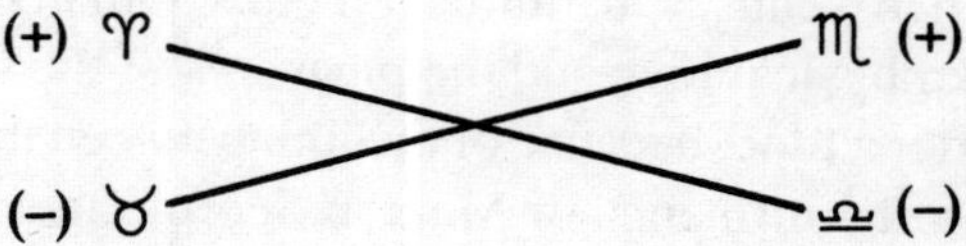

Figure 4

As you see, each axis connects a positive, masculine pole to a negative, feminine pole. In this case, Venus is the feminine pole which is linked to Mars, the masculine pole. When the masculine and feminine principles are in opposition to each other they do not remain passive; on the contrary, they have a mutually stimulating effect. Each is exalted by and provokes a reaction on the part of the other. Try this experiment: stare at something red for a few moments and then switch your gaze to a white surface and you will see that green appears. And vice versa, if you stare at something green, you will see red when you look away. Red is the colour of Mars and green is the colour of Venus and if you understand this phenomenon you will be better able to understand certain psychic manifestations. When you work with Taurus, this sign inevitably arouses its opposite, Scorpio, and vice versa: Scorpio arouses Taurus. When you work with Aries, you will necessarily trigger a reaction from Libra, and vice versa, for there is a link between these constellations.

When Venus is in Taurus it incites human beings to seek physical love and the pleasures of the senses and, after a time, because of the link between the two planets, the influence of Mars in Scorpio inevitably makes itself felt too, and this means quarrels, violence and destruction. Yes, those who abandon themselves to the frenzies of physical love end by becoming harsh and aggressive, even cruel; on the other hand, those who allow themselves to be ruled by violence and belligerence very soon become a prey to their sexual instincts. This is a phenomenon which is often seen in times of war.

When Venus manifests itself on the higher plane, however, as disinterested love, kindness, self-abnegation and beauty, Mars is also aroused and manifests itself, but no longer in destruction and upheavals. No, on the higher plane, Mars manifests itself by strengthening, sustaining and protecting all that is good in ourselves and others. This law is absolute. He who is inhabited by spiritual love cannot be drawn into violence; on the contrary, he attracts the positive, beneficial aspects of Mars. And if it is Mars that first manifests itself in you through your efforts of self-control, through your struggle for the mastery of your passions, then the love of Venus will come to dilate your soul and give you a foretaste of eternal life.

And now, let's study the sign of Scorpio. Scorpio corresponds to the eighth house of the Zodiac, the house of death. In his account of the creation of the world at the beginning of the Book of Genesis, Moses says that God placed Adam and Eve in a garden in which He had planted many different kinds of trees and gave them instructions concerning two of those trees: the Tree of Life and the Tree of the Knowledge of Good and Evil. 'And the Lord God commanded the man, saying, of every tree of the garden you may freely eat; but of the Tree of the Knowledge of Good and Evil you shall not eat, for in the day that you eat of it you shall surely die'. Don't you think that these are strange names for trees: the Tree of Life and the Tree of the Knowledge of Good and Evil? Actually, you must not take these trees to be realities of the vegetable kingdom; they are symbols of the regions of the universe. The Tree of Life is the symbol of the unity of life, of the plane on which polarization does not yet exist, that is to say, on the plane on which there is neither masculine nor feminine, neither light nor darkness. Whereas the other Tree represents the region of polarization, the plane on which creatures are necessarily subject to the alternation of day and night, of joy and sorrow, of all opposites.

God told Adam and Eve, 'The time will come when you will have the right to eat that fruit but, at the moment, you are too weak. If you ate it now, the contact with the forces it contains would kill you.' You will object that Adam and Eve did eat that fruit and yet continued to live. Yes, for the fact is that there is no such thing as death in nature: what we call death is simply an altered state of mind or of matter.

This changed state of mind undergone by Adam and Eve is indicated in Genesis by their sudden realization of their nudity. We are told that, when they lived happily in the Garden of Eden, 'They were both naked, the man and his wife, and were not ashamed'. And later, after they had eaten the forbidden fruit, 'The eyes of both of them were opened, and they knew that they were naked; and they sewed fig leaves together and made themselves coverings.' This sudden consciousness of their nakedness proves that a change of some kind had taken place within them. And this change was in their bodies: the subtle, luminous matter of which their bodies had been composed until then had congealed and become materialized so that they became aware of their nudity and felt the need to clothe themselves. When a being is made of pure light no one is going to ask whether he is naked or clothed: his form is fluid and his garments are indistinguishable from his body. But when he descends onto the level of physical matter, his form condenses and, if he has no physical clothes, he is seen to be naked.

Now, if we refer to Figure 2, we see that that which Initiatic Science has traditionally called 'the Fall' is, in fact, a descent onto the astral plane. Adam and Eve, who lived on the Buddhic plane, ruled by the higher aspects of Venus and Mars, fell to the astral plane, which is ruled by the lower aspects of these planets. In the Zodiac, the Tree of the Knowledge of Good and Evil is represented by the axis Taurus-Scorpio whereas the Tree of Life is represented by the axis Aries-Libra. Those whose lives are given over to sensuality and the passions eat the fruit of the Tree of the Knowledge of Good and Evil and die every day to the higher state, whereas those who are masters of their lower impulses eat the fruit of the Tree of Eternal Life in God's own Kingdom.

And now, if we re-read the letters to the Churches in Ephesus and Smyrna, we shall see that these explanations concerning the two axes, Aries-Libra and Taurus-Scorpio, throw a great deal of light on the text.

'To the Angel of the Church of Ephesus write, "These things says he who holds the seven stars in his right hand, who walks in the midst of the seven golden lampstands: I know your works, your labour, your patience (the qualities of work, courage and perseverance belong to the higher aspect of Mars). Nevertheless I have this against you, that you have left your first love (that is to say, the higher aspect of Venus). Remember therefore from where you have fallen; repent and do the first works (don't remain in the swamps of the astral plane; make the effort to get back the strength and spiritual love of the Buddhic plane). But this you have, that you hate the deeds of the Nicolaitans, which I also hate (Aries is herbivorous and the symbol of purity. The Nicolaitans were a heretical sect whose members took part in the banquets at which the flesh of animals that had been immolated in sacrifice was distributed). To him who overcomes I will give to eat from the tree of life, which is in the midst of the Paradise of God" (that is to say, the qualities and joys of divine love on the Buddhic plane).'

And to the Church in Smyrna it is said: 'I know your works, tribulation, and poverty although you are rich (Taurus corresponds to the second astrological house which is the house of wealth and prosperity. The poverty referred to, therefore, is the spiritual poverty of the Church of Smyrna which has fallen under the influence of the lower aspect of Venus in Taurus and of Mars in Scorpio, and the result is the tribulation that is mentioned for the second time). Indeed, the Devil is about to throw some of you into prison, that you may be tested, and you will have tribulation ten days. Be faithful unto death, and I will give you the crown of life. He who overcomes shall not be hurt by the second death' (No one can escape the first death, physical death, but he who wins the victory over his passions will escape the second death, spiritual death, inflicted by Scorpio).

Chapter Five

LETTER TO THE CHURCH IN PERGAMOS

'To the Angel of the Church in Pergamos write, "These things says he who has the sharp two-edged sword: I know your works, and where you dwell, where Satan's throne is. And you hold fast to my name, and did not deny my faith even in the days in which Antipas was my faithful martyr, who was killed among you, where Satan dwells. But I have a few things against you, because you have there those who hold the doctrine of Balaam, who taught Balak to put a stumbling block before the children of Israel, to eat things sacrificed to idols, and to commit sexual immorality. Thus you also have those who hold the doctrine of the Nicolaitans, which things I hate. Repent, or else I will come to you quickly and will fight against them with the sword of my mouth.

He who has an ear, let him hear what the Spirit says to the churches. To him who overcomes I will give some of the hidden manna to eat. And I will give him a white stone, and on the stone a new name written which no one knows except him who receives it".'

Revelations 2, 12-17

I want to restrict my comments today to the two promises at the end of this excerpt from the letter to the Angel of the Church in Pergamos. 'To him who overcomes I will give some of the hidden manna to eat. And I will give him a white stone, and on the stone a new name written which no one knows except him who receives it.'

There has already been a lot of discussion about this white stone. What can be so extraordinary about a white stone that it should be considered a fitting reward for someone who has won a victory? We are told that a name is written on it and from this we can conclude that it bears signs and inscriptions such as are found on a talisman or pantacle. Actually, a pantacle is not exactly the same thing as a talisman. A pantacle is an image - engraved on metal or stone, drawn on parchment or even embroidered on cloth - on which there is some writing. A talisman, on the other hand, is an object - a stone, flower, insect, ring or bracelet, etc. - which has been impregnated with a special force, either by nature or by someone who has great psychic power.

A lot of people would like to have a talisman that they could rely on to help and protect them and there is certainly nothing wrong in this, but don't imagine that it is so easy as all that to find a genuine talisman. All those stones, rings, crosses, etc., that you can buy in certain shops and that are 'guaranteed' to protect you from illness and win you love, fame and fortune - only the Lord knows what they will really do for you. It is not so easy to prepare a talisman. In the first place one has to be familiar with the laws of correspondence between physical objects and cosmic powers. Not only must you know which metal or stone is appropriate but you also have to know which signs and characters have the power to attract and hold beneficial forces.

Very often the names inscribed on talismans are in Hebrew. Why is this? It is because a cabbalist knows that each letter of the Hebrew alphabet corresponds to a particular geometrical form in nature and that behind each of these forms are certain active forces. Nature knows how to establish the link between its own forms and the letters that represent them and he who knows the invisible power to which each letter corresponds can, therefore, trigger the appropriate cosmic currents. In this way, by engraving or inscribing certain forms on a talisman, one establishes communication with the corresponding entities in the invisible world. Initiates seek to discover the correspondence between forces, forms and letters and to learn how to handle them in order to create beneficial contacts between Heaven and earth.

Actually, the work of the person who prepares a talisman is identical with that of nature, for nature fills stones, plants, animals and even men with a quintessence that can subsequently be drawn from them and when someone prepares a talisman he simply makes use of the natural energies present in all that exists. However, he must first know the laws involved and, also, he must never use those energies for egotistical, self-serving purposes. This is why, if you really want a talisman, you should find out who prepared it and be sure that it was someone who was pure, honest, upright and enlightened, otherwise the thing that you believed would be beneficial to you will be useless or even harmful. Yes, unfortunately, this also happens, for the nature and virtues of the elements that a person attracts from space can only be those that he already possesses.

It is also important to know the motives of someone who wants a talisman. Does he want its support in order to accomplish a disinterested work of light or in order to achieve personal success without effort? Unfortunately, it is this second reason that is most frequent; more often than not, greed and sloth underlie the desire for a talisman. Why should anyone study, reflect, meditate, pray and be vigilant when he can have a talisman to do the work for him? While it works, its owner can make the most of the advantages it obtains for him to do what he pleases and indulge in all the pleasures of life. No, no; that is not what a talisman is for and this is why a genuine magus will not give a talisman to everyone who asks for one. I have often refused to prepare a talisman for people - even though some were ready to pay me a great deal for it - because, knowing what they wanted it for, I knew that it would not only do them no good - quite the contrary, in fact - but that they might also cause harm to those around them.

I must also tell you that even the most powerful talisman can sometimes be totally ineffectual, because its potency depends on all kinds of other factors. Consider what the Spirit says to the Church in Pergamos: 'To him who overcomes I will give a white stone'. Yes, he will receive a white stone, that is true: but only after he has overcome. And what is it that he has to overcome? An enemy? A competitor? No; it is himself; his own weaknesses and passions and his own base inclinations. The message of the spirit is not that man will overcome thanks to the talisman he receives but that he must begin by acquiring the necessary virtues and qualities that will enable him to be victorious and only then will he be given the hidden manna and the white stone. The 'manna' is not really a food, nor is the 'white stone' a material stone; they are both symbols of the spiritual gifts that enable man to further his evolution. It is the virtues that are the only true food, the only true talisman.

The 'hidden manna', the food that bestows eternal life, is simply a state of consciousness that allows man to taste fulfilment, immensity and eternity. And the 'white stone' is the symbol of self-mastery, of the inner strength that comes from purity. According to the law of analogy, crystals and precious stones which are so pure and transparent, represent the highest sphere of the universe for, being linked to the Atmic plane, they have the power to condense within themselves the cosmic energy which we can then draw on and use for our own purposes. The 'white stone' is, therefore, the crystallization of the Atmic quintessence which is pure light.

And on this stone is written a name. What does this mean? In Initiatic Science, a name is of the utmost importance, for its function is to express, by means of its vibrations, the very essence of the being or object it designates. As soon as God had created the first man and woman He gave them their names and entrusted them with the task of giving names to the animals and plants. The name represents, sums up and contains the entity to which it belongs, and when a human being succeeds in attaining a higher level of consciousness he receives a new name. Yes, because he has been regenerated. This was how, as we read in Genesis, Abram became Abraham: 'Then Abram fell on his face, and God talked with him, saying: "As for Me, behold My covenant is with you, and you shall be a father of many nations. No longer shall your name be called Abram, but your name shall be Abraham; for I have made you a father of many nations"[1].' Similarly, when Saul was converted and ceased to persecute the Christians, he received the name of Paul.

The vibrations of the new name given to a

[1] Genesis 17, 3-5

regenerated human being express the quintessence of his spiritual reality. Every man and woman has a name that was given to them by their parents when they were born but, more often than not, this name does not mean much. The name a human being receives from Heavenly entities, however, corresponds exactly to what he is: it is a faithful expression of his deepest reality. And, in truth, only he can really know it, for it is an integral part of that reality.

Chapter Six

LETTER TO THE CHURCH IN LAODICEA

'And to the angel of the Church of the Laodiceans write, "These things says the Amen, the Faithful and True Witness, the Beginning of the creation of God: I know your works, that you are neither cold nor hot. I could wish you were cold or hot. So then, because you are lukewarm, and neither cold nor hot, I will spew you out of My mouth. Because you say, 'I am rich, have become wealthy, and have need of nothing' - and do not know that you are wretched, miserable, poor, blind and naked - I counsel you to buy from Me gold refined in the fire, that you may be rich; and white garments, that you may be clothed, that the shame of your nakedness may not be revealed; and anoint your eyes with eye salve, that you may see. As many as I love, I rebuke and chasten. Therefore be zealous and repent.

Behold, I stand at the door and knock. If anyone hears My voice and opens the door, I will come in to him and dine with him, and he with Me.

To him who overcomes I will grant to sit with Me on My throne, as I also overcame and sat down with My Father on His throne".'

Revelations 3, 14-21

'Because you are lukewarm, and neither cold nor hot, I will spew you out of My mouth.' Has anyone who has ever heard these words failed to be struck by them? For the last two thousand years they have been repeated over and over again and everyone believes that he understands them, because everyone knows what heat and cold are. Yes, everyone has experienced heat and cold and yet some further explanation is called for, because no one really understands their deepest meaning.

People often see coldness as a symbol of evil, of everything that contracts, congeals and paralyses, whereas heat symbolizes all that is good, beautiful, alive and generous and, on this basis, they conclude that the Spirit was saying, 'Put yourself on the side of either good or evil; don't waver between the two!' as though to be lukewarm were to be neither good nor evil. Well, there may be some truth in this interpretation, but it is incomplete.

The first thing we need to know is that there are two kinds of heat and cold. There is the heat that dilates, vivifies and ripens and there is the heat that burns and destroys and leaves only ashes. Then there is the cold that preserves what is good and provides excellent conditions for reflection and the cold that destroys life. These are the two kinds of heat and cold that we need to examine.

In very hot equatorial regions of the world, plant and animal life is abundant, exuberant and highly coloured. But it is also in these regions that the most dangerous animal species are to be found. As for the human population, their passions are ardent but they are also indolent and lazy. Heat is not conducive to work and discipline. Go to colder regions, however, and you will find that nature is less abundant and varied but that the people are more peaceful, more thoughtful and also more active. There are no great philosophers in hot countries; people are more concerned with eating, sleeping, loving and fighting whereas conditions in a cold climate encourage intellectual activity and oblige people to think and be inventive. On the other hand, the heart is not at ease in the cold and does not have the conditions it needs to develop. The heart needs warmth; it awakens and expands in the warmth whereas the intellect goes to sleep. Heat, therefore, stimulates men's passions and drives them to act without moderation or wisdom. This is why he needs the cold. But if the cold is too great he closes up and becomes distant, insensitive and proud. Symbolically you could say that the equator represents the stomach and sexual organs and the polar regions represent the head, the brain.

The cycle through which water goes in nature illustrates another aspect of this question of heat and cold. Water evaporates when it is heated by the sun's rays; in the upper atmosphere it is chilled and falls back to the mountain tops of earth in the form of snow. But it does not stay there. After a while, under the influence of the heat from the sun, the snow melts and flows into the valleys, once again, in the form of water, and the cycle begins all over again. As you see, nature uses this alternation of heat and cold, and Initiates, who observe nature very closely, have taken inspiration from it in their pedagogical methods.

When a Master sees that his disciples are becoming cold and icy, he sends them down into the valleys to get warm; that is to say, he counsels them to cultivate more love by mixing with others and getting involved in their lives. And when he sees others who are exposing themselves to too much heat he counsels them to rise as often as possible into the cooler air of the mountain heights. And what are these heights? They are meditation and prayer. In this way, disciples learn to use their powers of thought to rise above the conflagrations of the heart and, when they reach the heights and see their situation more clearly, they thank God that they have been rescued from the fire that threatened to consume them.

All those who are a prey to torments of the heart should use this method: they should rise to a higher level and, in this way, become wise and prudent. However, a disciple should not stay on the higher level indefinitely, otherwise he will become proud, distant and inaccessible to others. He must come down into the valley in order to help his brothers and sisters. It is not necessary to stay up on the mountain tops - symbolically speaking - for too long.

Look at what happens to a snake: in a warm climate it is extremely agile and can move very rapidly, so you can easily be bitten. But in a cold climate it becomes completely inoffensive. And, as we know, in each one of us dwells a live snake: our sexual energy. When the temperature begins to rise in man, this snake becomes so powerful that it is impossible to avoid being bitten. This is why we have to cool it off a little. Man's sexual energy is aroused by the fires of passion; it is rendered harmless by the cooler climate of reason.

And now, in the light of these explanations, the letter to the Church in Laodicea is beginning to be more intelligible. 'You are neither cold nor hot'; that is to say, 'you are neither up on the mountain nor down in the valley; you have neither wisdom nor love'. For this is what it means to be lukewarm: to possess neither wisdom nor love; and when a person possesses neither wisdom nor love he cannot possess truth. Take a very simple example from everyday life: if you put your left hand in a basin of hot water and your right hand in a basin of cold water and keep them there for a few minutes, the temperature of each hand will rise or fall until it matches that of the water. Then, if you remove both hands and dip them immediately into a third basin of lukewarm water, what impression will you have? Your left hand will give you a sensation of cold whilst your right hand will give you a sensation of warmth. You cannot, therefore, have an accurate idea of the temperature of the water in this third basin. Each of your hands has a different sensation depending on the difference between the hot or cold water and the lukewarm water. In the same way, you will never have an accurate notion of things if you content yourself with 'lukewarm' thoughts, feelings and actions. Those who dwell in lukewarmness will always be misled. This is why the Spirit says to the Church in Laodicea: 'Be hot or cold'.

And now let's get back to the two kinds of heat and cold that I mentioned a moment ago. There is one kind of heat that comes from the Sun and another that comes from Mars. There is one kind of cold that comes from Saturn and another that comes from Earth. The Sun represents the heat that gives life whereas Mars represents the all-consuming fire of passion. Saturn represents the coldness of wisdom and intelligence while Earth represents the coldness of separation and death. Coldness, therefore, is represented by Saturn and Earth and heat by the Sun and Mars. And the Moon represents lukewarmness. Yes, because everything that falls under the influence of the Moon becomes vague, colourless and insipid and when human beings are influenced by the Moon they are indolent, hesitant, indecisive and vague. You must not remain in a state of lukewarmness; you must work to become hot or cold (by which I mean, of course, the good aspect of heat and cold). To become cold you have to scale the heights, that is to say, reflect and meditate; and to become hot you have to join your brothers and sisters in the valleys. It is by means of wisdom that you can become cooler and by means of love that you become warmer.

But no one must be exclusively hot or cold for ever; if someone is cold he must also know how to become hot, and vice versa. It is in this constant movement, the constant alternation between the two poles, that a human being finds life and balance. He who stays permanently in the heat or the cold ceases to evolve; all progress is arrested. What do you do when you want to cook some vegetables? You put them in a saucepan and you put the saucepan on the fire. Yes, but you don't leave it there for ever; after a while, you remove it. Why don't you leave it to burn? Because you are wise. Similarly, it is good to feel love for someone but wisdom tells you that it is not good to go too far. If the temperature begins to rise within you because of a man or woman, don't leave the saucepan on the fire! You understand what I am saying, don't you? The heat of love is very welcome. Yes, but only if it is balanced by the coolness of wisdom.

Now let's get back to the question of the Zodiac. We have already spoken about the axis formed by each of the six pairs of diametrically opposite constellations (see Figures 3 and 4). These six axes are: Aries-Libra, Taurus-Scorpio, Gemini-Sagittarius, Cancer-Capricorn, Leo-Aquarius and Virgo-Pisces and, as we saw, the message of the Spirit to the Churches in Ephesus and Smyrna concerned the axes Aries-Libra and Taurus-Scorpio. Each of the Churches to which the Spirit sent a message has a special link with one of the axes of the Zodiac. You will be thinking that there are seven Churches, but not seven axes. Well, as a matter of fact, there are seven, but the seventh is not shown in the Zodiac. This is the axis that passes at right angles through the centre of the wheel of the Zodiac and it is the start of a new series of six principles.

There are several symbolic figures that represent a wheel and one of them is the winged wheel. In the figure of the winged wheel, the wings represent the seventh axis, the axis on which the wheel of the Zodiac turns in space. This seventh axis is the motive power of the six others. Then there are, also, the wheels seen by Ezekiel in his vision: 'Behold, a wheel was on the earth beside each living Creature with its four faces. The appearance of the wheels and their works was like the colour of beryl, and all four had the same likeness. The appearance of their works was, as it were, a wheel in the middle of a wheel. When they went, they went toward any one of four directions; they did not turn aside when they went. As for their rims, they were so high they were awesome; and their rims were full of eyes, all around the four of them.'[1] These four wheels represent the Zodiac.

And now we can go back and take another look at what the Spirit said to the Church in Laodicea and you will see that it can be interpreted with reference to the axis Aquarius-Leo. 'You are neither cold nor hot. I counsel you to buy from Me gold refined in the fire, that you may be rich; and white garments, that you may be clothed, that the shame of your nakedness may not be revealed; and anoint your eyes with eye salve, that you may see. As many as I love, I rebuke and chasten'.

Leo is a fire sign and it is the fifth astrological house, the house of the Sun, and it corresponds to the hottest months of the year, July and August. Leo represents the heart and the heart is associated with heat, blood and life. This is the cosmic heart, the heart of God from which come all creatures and all that exists in the universe. The fifth astrological house is the house of love, children and all forms of creation. The other pole of this axis is Aquarius which is ruled by Saturn, and Saturn reigns over winter. Aquarius is represented as an old man, old man Saturn (although Saturn is not the only ruler of Aquarius; there is also Uranus), who possesses wisdom and who, symbolically, pours out water for all creatures. The two poles of this axis, therefore, are love and wisdom, the heat of the valley and the

[1] Ezekiel 1, 15-18.

cold of the mountain peaks.

The letter to the Church in Laodicea speaks of gold, white garments and eye-salve (collyrium): what do these mean? Gold, according to the alchemists, is closely related to the sun: it is a condensation of the sun's rays. Gold purified by fire represents all the beneficial forces issuing from Leo, the heart of the universe. Gold is the love of this heart. As a matter of fact, the etymology of the words lion (Leo), heart and love, makes it very clear that there is a connection between them. The Hebrew for heart is *lev*, and for lion, *lavi*; in Bulgarian and Russian, the word for lion is *lèv* and for love, *lubov*, and the same root is found in the English word 'love' and the German *Liebe* (love) and *Löwe* (lion).

And what of the 'white garments'? White garments are often mentioned in the Apocalypse and are, of course, symbolic. White is the synthesis of all the other colours and, in the language of Initiatic Science, to have a white garment means to possess the light, that is to say, to possess wisdom; for wisdom is the synthesis of all the virtues, just as white is the synthesis of all the colours. These spiritual 'garments' are what we also know as the 'aura', and it is by our aura, the spiritual garment woven by wisdom, that the Invisible World recognizes us[2].

[2] See *Complete Works*, vol. 6, chap. 12

'An eye salve with which to anoint your eyes': the eye-salve or collyrium referred to here is Uranus, truth; for truth is related to the eyes. In the ancient Initiations, Uranus was depicted as an eye hovering over the ocean. You must not think that Antiquity did not know of the existence of this planet; Sir William Herschel was not the first to discover it: it was known to the world of Antiquity by its Greek name of Ouranos, meaning Heaven or sky.

Thus, the Sun gives us life and love; Saturn gives us the garment of wisdom, and Uranus enables us to see the truth. Although the Church in Laodicea believes that it is rich (You say, 'I am rich, have become wealthy, and have need of nothing'), the Spirit knows that that is not so. On the contrary, it is 'wretched, miserable, poor, blind and naked' and the Spirit counsels it to buy gold, white garments and an eye-salve. This shows us that, in order to obtain love, wisdom and truth, we have to work with the Aquarius-Leo axis, otherwise we shall be poor, naked and blind for ever.

The Spirit also tells the Church, 'As many as I love (Leo), I rebuke and chasten (Aquarius).' The one who loves is the Sun and the Sun is domiciled in Leo; the one who chastens is Saturn but also Uranus, for the coming of Uranus is accompanied by great upheavals, and both planets are domiciled in Aquarius. If Heaven, which loves us, chastens us, It does so through the circumstances and events of our destiny which is ruled by Saturn. When we feel that we are being chastened by Saturn, therefore, we must remember that it is God who is manifesting Himself through him[3]. If we want to be loved, we must dwell both in Leo and in Aquarius, between Saturn, the Old Adam, and the Sun, Christ, he who was born of the tribe of Judah, son of Jacob. Jacob had twelve sons, the ancestors of the twelve tribes of Israel, and each of these tribes is related to one of the signs of the Zodiac. The tribe of Judah corresponds to Leo, and Jesus, the Christ, was born to the tribe of Judah.

The Spirit also says, 'To him who overcomes I will grant to sit with Me on My throne, as I also overcame and sat down with My Father on His throne'. There is no throne other than that of Leo, on which is seated the Sun, Christ. Symbolically speaking, Christ is the Sun, the heart that pours out its blood - its love - into the universe. And this means, therefore, that he who overcomes hatred and death (inner coldness) will reign on the throne of God.

[3] Saturn is the planet of the Sephirah Binah and Binah is ruled by the Twenty-four Elders, the Lords of Destiny. See also the following chapter.

Chapter Seven

THE TWENTY-FOUR ELDERS AND THE FOUR HOLY LIVING CREATURES

‘After these things I looked, and behold, a door standing open in Heaven. And the first voice which I heard was like a trumpet speaking with me, saying, “Come up here, and I will show you things which must take place after this.” Immediately I was in the Spirit; and behold, a throne set in Heaven, and One sat on the throne. And He who sat there was like a jasper and a sardius stone in appearance; and there was a rainbow around the throne, in appearance like an emerald. Around the throne were twenty-four thrones, and on the thrones I saw twenty-four Elders sitting, clothed in white robes; and they had crowns of gold on their heads. And from the throne proceeded lightnings, thunderings, and voices. And there were seven lamps of fire burning before the throne, which are the seven Spirits of God.

Before the throne there was a sea of glass, like crystal. And in the midst of the throne, and around the throne, were four Living Creatures full of eyes in front and in back. The first Living Creature was like a lion, the second Living Creature like a calf, the third Living Creature had a face like a man, and the fourth Living Creature was like a flying eagle. And the four Living Creatures, each having six wings, were full of eyes around and within. And they do not rest day or night, saying:

"Holy, holy, holy, Lord God Almighty, Who was and is and is to come!'

Revelations, 4, 1-8

St John's visions, first of the Twenty-four Elders seated on the thrones and then of the four Holy Living Creatures, cannot be understood unless one is familiar with the cabbalistic Tree of Life, the Sephirotic Tree. A door was opened in Heaven, and the voice that had already spoken to St John now told him 'Come up here'. The description of the Twenty-four Elders that follows reveals that St John was raised to the third Sephirah, Binah; the Sephirah to which is attached the Angelic order of the Aralim which are known in the Christian religion as the Thrones. After this he has a vision of the four Holy Living Creatures and his description of what he sees makes it clear that he had been taken up to the level of the first Sephirah, Kether; to which is attached the Angelic order of the Seraphim, the Hayot Ha-Kadosh. St John, therefore, was transported in the spirit to the most sublime heights of creation.

St John tells us that the Twenty-four Elders and the four Holy Living Creatures stand before the throne of God, blessing Him and singing His praises, but he neither describes God nor even names Him.

He simply says, 'Behold, a throne set in Heaven, and One sat on the throne. And He who sat there was like a jasper and a sardius stone in appearance'. The only way to convey an idea of God is to use an image of light: flashes of lightning proceeded from the throne and seven lamps burned before it; seven lamps that represent the seven spirits of God.

This imagery is also found in the *Zohar*, in which we read: 'Seven lights are there in the Most-High, and therein dwells the Ancient of Ancients, the Secret of all Secrets, the Hidden of all the Hidden Ones: Ain Soph.' Ain Soph (meaning limitless, without end) or Ain Soph Aur (limitless light) is the name that cabbalists use for the Absolute Godhead, the most sublime quintessence of the Deity, and the seven spirits are the seven lights or rays: red, orange, yellow, green, blue, indigo and violet. The colours of the spectrum have symbolic value: they represent the first differentiation of primordial Light, God. It is because light can be split up into seven colours that seven is the number of wholeness, totality, and there are many mentions of this number in Revelations: the seven Churches, seven seals, seven lampstands, seven stars, and so on.

The Twenty-four Elders seated before the throne of God are clothed in white robes and wear crowns of gold on their heads. The white robes and the crowns of gold both symbolize the spiritual light that emanates from these sublime entities. The white robe represents the Body of Glory; and the crown,

TREE OF LIFE

1 EHIEH
Kether - *Crown*
Metatron
Hayot Ha-Kadosh - *Seraphim*
Rashith Ha-Galgalim - *First Swirlings (Neptune)*
♆

3 JEHOVAH
Binah - *Intelligence*
Tsaphkiel
Aralim - *Thrones*
Shabbathai - *Saturn*
♄

2 YAH
Chokmah - *Wisdom*
Raziel
Ophanim - *Cherubim*
Mazloth - *The Zodiac (Uranus)*
♅

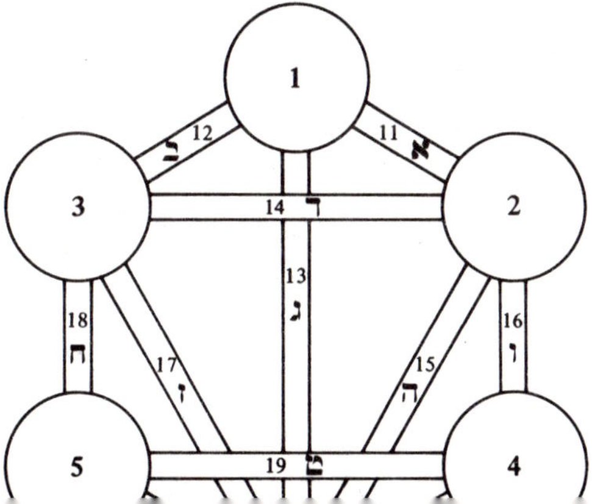

5 ELOHIM GIBOR
Geburah - *Severity*
Khamaël
Seraphim - *Powers*

4 EL
Chesed - *Mercy*
Tsadkiel
Hashmalim - *Dominations*

Hod - *Glory*
Raphaël
Bnei Elohim - *Archangels*
Kokab - *Mercury*
☿

9 CHADAI-EL-HAI
Yesod - *The Foundation*
Gabriel
Kerubim - *Angels*
Levanah - *Moon*
☽

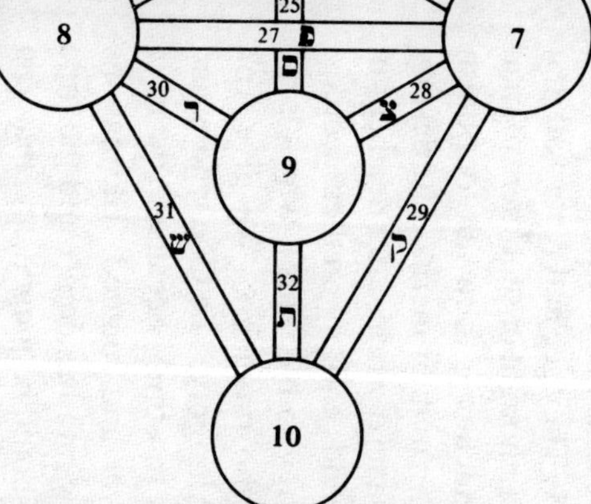

Netzach - *Victory*
Haniel
Elohim - *Principalities*
Noga - *Venus*
♀

6 ELOHA va DAATH
Tiphareth - *Beauty*
Mikhaël
Melachim - *Virtues*
Chemesh - *Sun*
☉

10 ADONAI MALEK
Malkuth - *The Kingdom*
Uriel (Sandalfon)
Ishim - *Beatified Souls*
Cholem Ha-Yesodoth - *Earth*
♁

because it is something that is placed above the head, represents an extremely subtle matter which is no longer the physical body, the head itself, but an emanation of the spirit, of the wisdom and omnipotence of the spirit. This crown is of gold; and gold, according to spiritual symbolism, is simply condensed light.

The Cabbalah represents the Twenty-four Elders as the Lords of Destiny. They see and record all that men do; not a single act, thought or sentiment of man escapes them. Their function is to reward or punish human beings according to their merits. The destiny of a human being in the next world, after death, or in a later incarnation depends entirely on their decrees; and their decrees are irrevocable. This is why it is the Twenty-four Elders who proclaim, 'We give You thanks, O Lord God Almighty, The One who is and who was and who is to come, because You have taken your great power and reigned. The nations were angry, and your wrath has come, and the time of the dead, that they should be judged, and that You should reward your servants the prophets and the saints, and those who fear your name, small and great, and should destroy those who destroy the earth'[1].

The four Holy Living Creatures that dwell in the Sephirah Kether, on the other hand, are the four principles of matter. The Absolute God is an entity

[1] Revelations 11, 17-18.

that cannot be conceived or grasped by man; we can only know Him through His manifestation, and the manifestation of God is the matter that He has brought forth from His own Being. Matter is divine in origin and on this sublime level of purity and subtlety it is inconceivable and incomprehensible to man, for it is one with the spirit. It is this primordial matter that is symbolized by the four Holy Living Creatures, the roots of the four elements. The calf represents earth; the eagle, water; the man, air, and the lion, fire. These are the same Creatures that were seen by Ezekiel in his vision[2]. They are so highly exalted that it is they who are entrusted with the task of glorifying the Lord. Night and day the Lord is glorified by the Seraphim who repeat without ceasing, 'Holy, holy, holy, Lord God Almighty, Who was and is and is to come.' They themselves are called holy and they never cease praising the holiness of the Lord.

Why is it that the highest form of praise that a creature can offer his Creator is to proclaim His holiness, His sanctity? Of course, in common parlance, the words 'saint' and 'sanctity', 'holy' and 'holiness' have been used so indiscriminately that their true significance has been lost. Sanctity is, in reality, a quality of light. There are words in some Slavic languages that express exactly this correspondence. In Bulgarian, for example, *svetia*

[2] Ezekiel, 1, 4-14.

means a saint and *svetost* means sanctity, while *svetlina* means light, and *svet* means the world. The link between sanctity and light is obvious. Sanctity, therefore, is *par excellence* the attribute of God, because He is pure light and it was by light that He created the world. A human being can be said to be holy only to the extent to which he possesses the light that shines on the higher mental plane, that is to say, true intelligence, true wisdom.

The four Holy Living Creatures represent the four elements, therefore, but you must not confuse these elements with the elements that constitute our universe; they are far above and beyond the reach of our five senses or even of the most sophisticated instruments. The four elements known to us as fire, air, water and earth, are no more than a pale reflection, a crude condensation of the matter that exists on high in the Sephirah Kether. This is why a human being must have attained an exceptionally high degree of evolution in order to have access to Kether. Very few have ever reached this level and, of those who have, most have never been able to reintegrate their physical body. The Sephirah Kether is a region in which all forms cease to exist; this is why those who attain this level disappear: they are consumed immediately, on contact; they themselves become fire. The few very rare beings who have returned to earth after attaining Kether, therefore, were only able to do so thanks to a special grace from Heaven which allowed them to absorb an element that has the property of protecting the physical body.

If St John did not disappear during the ecstasies he describes in Revelations, it is because he had received that element. The little book that the Angel gave him to eat, saying, 'It will make your stomach bitter, but it will be as sweet as honey in your mouth'[3] symbolizes this element that is capable of preserving the physical body. The Prophet Ezekiel also spoke of a little book that the Angel gave him to eat[4], and the live coal with which one of the Seraphim touched the lips of Isaiah[5] is also a symbol of that element.

The Seraphim, the Angels of the four elements, are, therefore, the most exalted in the Angelic hierarchy and it is only very exceptionally that human beings have managed to reach them. This is why, when we invoke the angels of air, water, earth or fire, we can only reach the luminous entities that rule the physical water, wind, fire and earth of our human experience. You must not confuse the angels that preside over the four elements of our physical world with the four great Angels that are the very principles of matter. The fire of our human experience is not true fire; true fire, air, water and earth exist on a higher plane and when they intervene on earth they do so through the agency of intermediate entities under their command. This is why, when St John describes the cataclysms

[3] Revelations 10, 9.

[4] Ezekiel 3, 1-3.

[5] Isaiah 6, 6-7.

befalling the world, he shows how the four Holy Living Creatures commanded the elements of the physical plane.

'Now I saw when the Lamb opened one of the seals; and I heard one of the four Creatures saying with a voice like thunder, "Come and see". And I looked, and behold, a white horse. And he who sat on it had a bow.

When He opened the second seal, I heard the second Living Creature saying, "Come and see". And another horse, fiery red, went out. And it was granted to the one who sat on it to take peace from the earth.

When He opened the third seal, I heard the third Living Creature say, "Come and see". And I looked, and behold, a black horse, and he who sat on it had a pair of scales in his hand.

When He opened the fourth seal, I heard the voice of the fourth Living Creature saying, "Come and see". And I looked, and behold, a pale horse. And the name of him who sat on it was Death, and Hades followed with him. And power was given to them over a fourth of the earth, to kill with sword, with hunger, with death, and by the beasts of the earth'[6].

The four horses with the four Horsemen on their backs are a symbol of the cataclysms ordained by the four great Angels of the elements on high, for these

[6] Revelations 6, 1-8.

Angels are so powerful that the merest sign from them sets in motion other forces which devastate the face of the earth. Why can't human beings understand that everything they do entails certain consequences and that they cannot continue to transgress the laws of nature and interfere with the work of the elements with impunity? By their actions and, also, by their thoughts and feelings and their anarchical attitude, they exasperate the forces of nature and, in the long run, these forces react and move to restore order. Nature is not something inert and insensate, and human beings don't have the right to do whatever they please with her; when they exceed the bounds of what she is prepared to put up with, she retaliates.

But if this is true for the earth, it is also true for every individual. If you are incapable of maintaining harmonious relations with the four elements within you (with earth, your physical body; with water, your heart; with air, your intellect, and with fire, your soul and spirit), you will be obliged to live through great tribulations. I have already given you methods to use in your work with the four elements; try to look them up and begin to apply them[7]. Get into the habit of making contact with the angels of the four elements and you will begin to feel that, at last, you are entering into the splendour of harmony.

[7] See *Complete Works*, vol. 13, chap 6.

Chapter Eight

THE SCROLL AND THE LAMB

‘And I saw in the right hand of Him who sat on the throne a scroll written inside and on the back, sealed with seven seals. Then I saw a strong Angel proclaiming with a loud voice, “Who is worthy to open the scroll and to loose its seals?” And no one in Heaven or on the earth or under the earth was able to open the scroll, or to look at it. So I wept much, because no one was found worthy to open and read the scroll, or to look at it. But one of the Elders said to me, “Do not weep. Behold the Lion of the tribe of Judah, the Root of David, has prevailed to open the scroll and to loose its seven seals.”

And I looked, and behold, in the midst of the throne and of the four Living Creatures, and in the midst of the Elders, stood a Lamb as though it had been slain, having seven horns and seven eyes, which are the seven Spirits of God sent out into all the earth. Then He came and took the scroll out of the right hand of Him who sat on the throne.

Now when He had taken the scroll, the four Living Creatures and the twenty-four Elders fell down before the Lamb, each having a harp, and golden bowls full of incense, which are the prayers of the saints. And they sang a new song, saying: "You are worthy to take the scroll, and to open its seals; for You were slain, and have redeemed us to God by your blood out of every tribe and tongue and people and nation".'

Revelations 5, 1-9

In describing his vision of the four Holy Living Creatures and the Twenty-four Elders, St John disclosed the mysteries of the Sephiroth Kether and Binah. His next vision, that of the slain Lamb standing in the midst of the four Holy Living Creatures and the Twenty-four Elders who proclaim that He alone is worthy to open the scroll, introduces us into the mysteries of the second Sephirah, Chokmah.

Chokmah is the region of Christ, the Son, the second Person of the Trinity, the Logos, the Word uttered by the Father at the beginning. All the elements by means of which the world was created exist in Chokmah and these elements are symbolized by the twenty-two letters of the Hebrew alphabet. Chokmah is the cosmic alphabet with which the book of Creation was written. This is why St John says, at the beginning of his Gospel: 'In the beginning was the Word, and the Word was with God, and the Word was God. All things were made through Him, and without Him nothing that was made was made'. The Word is Christ, He who sits at the right hand of the Father. It is He, the Lion of Judah[1], who has conquered the right to open the scroll; it is He, also, who appears to St John in the form of a sacrificial Lamb, for the Lamb is another image of the Christ, the Son of God, immolated before the creation of the world[2].

The seven horns of the Lamb are the seven rays, for horns are a symbolic representation of the light that radiates from the head of a spiritual being. This is why Moses and other Initiates are often depicted with horns.

Christ is the Divine Lamb, the spirit of love that attracts, draws together and sustains all things. And it is He, this spirit of love, that is the bedrock and foundation of creation; it is He that sacrificed himself so that the matter of creation should be impregnated with the divine fluid of his blood. It is He that is the unifying bond, the link, the cement that ensures the cohesion of the universe, that binds together all the atoms, molecules and 'letters' of this immense Book. Everywhere, in the stones of the earth and the stars in the sky, it is this love that holds the structure together. Love is the most powerful force in the universe and this is why love alone is worthy to read the secrets of the universe.

There is a tradition according to which the

[1] Concerning the link between the lion and Christ, see chap. 6.

[2] See Revelations 13, 8.

Archangel Raziel, who is the Archangel of Chokmah, gave Adam the book that contains all the secrets of the universe but that, after the Fall, it was taken away from him. The Cabbalah is an attempt to rediscover the secrets contained in that book.

As I have already said, no one can decipher the Apocalypse if he is not familiar with the Initiatic tradition. Alchemy, astrology, magic, the Cabbalah and even the Tarot (the Tarot cards comprise a précis of a science that dates back many thousands of years) are all necessary in order to interpret the imagery of the Apocalypse.

The second trump of the Tarot, for instance, known as the Female Pope, represents a seated female figure with an open book in her lap which is partly concealed by a fold of her cloak. This open book expresses duality (the two halves of the book), whereas the closed book is the One, the non-manifested, the Absolute. The open book is Two, the One that has accepted to be polarized into positive and negative in order to be manifested. And it is this manifestation, this polarization that Initiates call Nature.

The Female Pope holding the open book in her lap, therefore, is Mother Nature and the book is the summary of all that she is. Yes, the book in which God has written all His secrets is Nature, the Cosmic Woman, Isis, and only an Initiate is worthy to strip away her veils in order to decipher her mysteries.

Chapter Nine

THE HUNDRED AND FORTY-FOUR THOUSAND SERVANTS OF GOD

'After these things I saw four Angels standing at the four corners of the earth, holding the four winds of earth, that the wind should not blow on the earth, on the sea, or on any tree. Then I saw another Angel ascending from the east, having the seal of the living God. And he cried with a loud voice to the four Angels to whom it was granted to harm the earth and the sea, saying, "Do not harm the earth, the sea, or the trees until we have sealed the servants of our God on their foreheads." And I heard the number of those who were sealed. One hundred and forty-four thousand of all the tribes of the children of Israel were sealed:

Of the tribe of Judah twelve thousand were sealed; of the tribe of Reuben twelve thousand were sealed; of the tribe of Gad twelve thousand were sealed; of the tribe of Asher twelve thousand were sealed; of the tribe of Naphtali twelve thousand were sealed; of the tribe of Manasseh twelve thousand were sealed; of the tribe of Simeon twelve thousand were sealed; of the tribe of Levi twelve thousand were sealed; of the tribe of Issachar twelve thousand were sealed; of the tribe of Zebulun twelve thousand were sealed; of the tribe of Joseph twelve thousand were sealed; of the tribe of Benjamin twelve thousand were sealed.

Revelations 7, 1-8.

As I have already told you, the interpretation of the Apocalypse requires a knowledge of various other disciplines: alchemy, astrology, the Cabbalah, etc. Without this knowledge one would inevitably go seriously astray. A great many people have believed, and indeed still do believe, that fire from Heaven will, one day, fall on the earth and only the hundred and forty-four thousand elect will be spared! There are several billion people on earth - is it possible that only a hundred and forty-four thousand are destined to escape this dreadful retribution? What torture, what anguish for each of us to think that we have such a slim chance of being spared! But, once again, we have to realize that this passage is symbolic and in order to interpret it we must call on some notions of astrology.

It says, 'After these things I saw four Angels standing at the four corners of the earth, holding the four winds of earth.' The four corners of the earth at which the Angels are standing are the four cardinal points of space within which lies the circle of the Zodiac. And the Zodiac is represented in this passage by the twelve tribes of Israel, that is to say, the twelve sons of Jacob[1]. Remember the lecture I gave you, years ago, in which I explained the correspondence between the twelve labours of Hercules, the twelve sons of Jacob and the twelve constellations of the Zodiac.

One night, after leaving his father's house, Jacob lay down on the ground and slept with his head on a stone. While he was asleep he saw a ladder between earth and Heaven on which Angels were going up and down. The Lord stood above the ladder and spoke to Jacob, saying, 'I am the Lord God of Abraham your father and the God of Isaac; the land on which you lie I will give to you and your descendants. Also your descendants shall be as the dust of the earth; you shall spread abroad to the west and the east, to the north and the south; and in you and in your seed all the families of the earth shall be blessed'[2]. The descendants of Jacob, therefore, are the twelve tribes of Israel which make up, symbolically, the People of God, and these twelve tribes are related to the twelve constellations of the Zodiac. The circle of the Zodiac is an image of the totality of space and within that totality each constellation has its own well-defined qualities and functions. As I have already shown you, Jacob's last words to his twelve sons (Chapter 49 of Genesis) clearly show the relationship of each one to a particular sign of the Zodiac.

[1] In the Book of Genesis, Jacob is also called Israel.
[2] Genesis 28, 13-14.

The importance of the number twelve is particularly obvious in this passage of Revelations. Twelve thousand from each of the twelve tribes were marked with the seal, giving a total of a hundred and forty-four thousand. Great importance is attached to the number twelve, also, in the description of the Heavenly Jerusalem at the end of Revelations. The New Jerusalem that comes down from Heaven has twelve foundations and twelve gates guarded by twelve Angels; its length and breadth are of twelve thousand furlongs, its walls are one hundred and forty-four cubits and on its gates are written the names of the twelve tribes of Israel. There is a close link, therefore, between the hundred and forty-four thousand elect and the New Jerusalem. They are two symbolic representations of the perfect life, the first in the form of the assembly of the servants of God and the second in the form of a city. A city is a collectivity of individual beings and in that city each individual can be seen as a dwelling, a construction. This was the notion that Jesus was expressing also when he said, 'You are the temple of the living God'.

He who sincerely wants to make progress sees a vast range of activities opening before him, activities which are represented symbolically by the twelve labours of Hercules which are also linked to the twelve signs of the Zodiac. The disciple has a long route to run, therefore, but it is a route that will enable him, little by little, to open the twelve gates[3] and to transform himself into the New Jerusalem, the city of light in which there is neither darkness nor illness nor death.

And now it is time to look at the question of the 'seal': what exactly is the seal on the forehead, the sign that marks out the righteous? Those who are chosen, the elect, bear a sign, that is true; but it is not an outward sign stamped arbitrarily on their foreheads by an Angel. Every human being marks himself with this sign by means of his own work and his own spiritual elevation. For, as I have so often told you, everything we do is recorded and our actions, sentiments and thoughts all leave traces, not only on our surroundings but also and above all on us. Our whole being is impregnated, moulded and fashioned by the manifestations of our psychic life. Yes, this is a law: every time we manifest kindness, justice, patience, love, and so on, these virtues are engraved within us; in fact, not only are they engraved within us but they also create, as it were, a magnetic field which attracts beneficial forces that gather round us for our protection. It is in this way that we can say that an Angel places a seal on our foreheads.

The system followed in the Divine School is exactly the same as that followed in the schools of this world: when a student passes his exams he is given a diploma which opens the doors of

[3] See chap 17, (iii), *The Gates of Pearl*.

opportunity to him. In the same way, when you pass the tests of life successfully you receive a diploma; but that diploma is not written on paper like those you get at a university and which can fade or be torn, burned or stolen. The diploma you receive from this School is written on the subtle plane, on your face, on your body, on your whole being, and no one can ever take it away from you. In fact, the spirits of nature recognize, appreciate and welcome you because they can read what is written on your diploma and, wherever you go, they see it and hasten to help and protect you. Yes, it is this living diploma of powerful, luminous emanations that is the seal that marks the foreheads of the Servants of God.

So it is quite useless to worry about whether or not you will be one of the hundred and forty-four thousand elect! The only thing you have to do is work. The grace of God does not fall by chance on just anybody; only on those who have earned it by their spiritual work[4].

[4] See *Complete Works*, vol. 26, chap. 5 (v).

Chapter Ten

THE WOMAN AND THE DRAGON

'Now a great sign appeared in heaven: a woman clothed with the sun, with the moon under her feet, and on her head a garland of twelve stars. Then being with child, she cried out in labour and in pain to give birth. And another sign appeared in heaven: behold, a great, fiery red dragon having seven heads and ten horns, and seven diadems on his heads. His tail drew a third of the stars of heaven and threw them to the earth. And the dragon stood before the woman who was ready to give birth, to devour her child as soon as it was born. And she bore a male child who was to rule all nations with an iron rod. And her child was caught up to God and to His throne, Then the woman fled into the wilderness, where she has a place prepared by God, that they should feed her there one thousand two hundred and sixty days.'

Revelations 12, 1-6

This text can be compared to the passage in Genesis in which the serpent succeeds in tempting Eve to sin by eating the forbidden fruit. In the symbolism of the Sephirotic Tree of Life, Eve, the feminine principle, corresponds to the Sephirah Yesod, the Moon (see the Tree of Life, pp. 92-93). Now the region of Yesod is immediately next to that of Malkuth, the Earth, and if it is not very closely allied to Tiphareth, the Sun, it will be open to the influence of terrestrial and even subterranean forces for, under the earth, dwell the Kliphot, the dark Sephiroth, the forces of evil symbolized by the serpent or dragon. This is what happened to Eve: if the serpent succeeded in slipping into her and seducing her, that is to say, in dragging her down to its own subterranean regions, it was because she was not closely united to Tiphareth, the Sun[1].

We can see that the woman described by St John, on the other hand, has succeeded in rising above Yesod - for she has the moon under her feet - and has reached the realm of Tiphareth - for she is clothed with the sun. Also, the garland of stars on her head means that she is bathed in the light emanating from the first Sephiroth. Standing before that woman is a dragon with ten horns (the ten dark Sephiroth, also known as the Kliphot), and seven heads (the lower manifestations of the seven planets) crowned with seven diadems. The dragon represents the reverse side of the Tree of Life. There are princes of darkness just as there are princes of light and this is why the dragon wears the seven diadems. But for all

[1] See *Complete Works*, vol. 32, chap. 6, 'The Fall and Redemption of Man'.

its great might, it is unable to triumph over the woman crowned with stars; in contrast to Eve, she escapes his clutches.

As we have seen, the woman is pregnant and the dragon is waiting for her to give birth so that it can devour her child. Symbolically, this child represents the coming of a new era while the dragon represents the forces of darkness that oppose this new era because they oppose the evolution of mankind. This is why they are lying in wait to devour the child as soon as it is born. The same idea is expressed in a later passage[2] which describes the great Harlot sitting on the scarlet beast with seven heads and ten horns like the dragon. The symbolism is the same: the world of darkness (represented by the demonic Sephiroth and the great Harlot) wages war against the world of light (represented by the higher Sephiroth and the Woman with the crown of stars).

Perhaps you are wondering why the figure of a woman is involved in both instances. The answer is that it is the feminine principle that holds the key to material realization, whether of good or of evil. The function of woman is to bring children into the world but a 'child' can also be a materialization on another plane, on the psychic or spiritual plane, for the same laws apply on all planes. It is in woman's nature to emanate particles of a very subtle nature, an etheric

[2] Revelations 17, 1-7.

form of matter, which can be used to incarnate and give body to ideas and plans.

It is up to women, therefore, to choose which ideas they want to see materialized. On the forehead of the great Harlot is written a name: 'Babylon the Great, the Mother of Harlots and of the Abominations of the Earth'. This image of the Harlot with the inscription on her forehead makes very clear the nature of the designs that she was bent on carrying out. Do the women of the world want to ally themselves with her in the accomplishment of those designs? They must realize that, depending on the orientation they choose, the salvation or the destruction of mankind is in their hands. Yes, women must become conscious of their immense power and understand that, just as there is only one woman in the higher world of archetypes, Cosmic Woman, and that she is clothed with the sun and crowned with stars, they too have the power to unite to form only one woman who will bring into the world the new life symbolized in Revelations by the descent of the Heavenly Jerusalem.

So many religious, spiritual men have shunned and despised women without realizing that it was precisely this attitude that made them incapable of bringing about the Kingdom of God! Yes, they will perhaps be infuriated to hear me say this, but it is the truth: many of them have spoken of woman as an inferior being afflicted with every vice, a creature of the Devil from whom they had to flee. They never realized that this attitude had a very negative influence on women. By constantly accusing them of being frivolous, flirtatious, spendthrift, unscrupulous, seductive, devious, etc., they only succeeded in creating conditions that would make them so. Some have even gone so far as to see all women as the incarnation of the Harlot with the inscription 'Bablyon the Great, Source of all Abominations' on her forehead, whereas, if women are made aware of their powers and are given the right conditions, they can become the Woman clothed in the sun and with a garland of stars on her head who will give birth to the Kingdom of God, the New Jerusalem.

There! Never forget that the Kingdom of God on earth can only be brought into being by women, for only woman possesses the matter needed to embody it. What a lot of mental attitudes still need to be changed!

Chapter Eleven

THE ARCHANGEL MIKHAEL CASTS OUT THE DRAGON

‘And war broke out in heaven: Mikhaël and his angels fought against the dragon; and the dragon and his angels fought, but they did not prevail, nor was a place found for them in heaven any longer. So the great dragon was cast out, that serpent of old, called the Devil and Satan, who deceives the whole world; he was cast to the earth, and his angels were cast out with him’.

Revelations 12, 7-10

The dragon is the name that tradition has always given to the cosmic principle of evil. This collective entity has also been depicted as an army of rebellious angels who rose up against God under the influence of their leader, Lucifer. It is this army of evil that is opposed by the Heavenly hosts under the leadership of the Archangel Mikhaël.

Why Mikhaël? Tradition tells us that when Lucifer declared himself to be God’s equal and attempted to dethrone Him, another Archangel stood up to him and cried out against such pride, saying, ‘*Mi* (who) *ka* (like) *El* (God)?’ that is to say, ‘Who is like God?’. Thenceforth he was called Mikhaël and placed at the head of the Heavenly hosts. In the Sephirotic Tree of Life, Mikhaël is the Archangel of the Sephirah Tiphareṭh, the Sephirah of the sun, the light that opposes darkness.

There have always been men in the world who have had the courage to throw themselves into a struggle to the death against the dragon but, to this day, none have vanquished it, for this battle is not the province of human beings: they have neither the stature, nor the breadth of vision, neither the power nor the methods required to defeat the dragon. Only a Heavenly entity, the Archangel Mikhaël, is capable of conquering the dragon. All those who have set out to make war against evil have themselves been vanquished, for evil is an extremely powerful cosmic force. It is a mistake to think, as some have done, that the powers of evil are as great as those of good and that the Devil is strong enough to stand up to God for ever. No, but where human beings are concerned it is true: the Devil is invincible.

You will ask, 'But does this mean that there is nothing we can do?' Yes, there is something you can do: you can enrol every day in the army of good, in the army of the children of God. And the day that army is sufficiently strong in numbers, the entities of darkness will be vanquished. The powers of darkness are free to do their evil work only because they are sustained by the greed and ignoble appetites of human beings. But the day will come when they will be defeated and bound hand and foot by the cosmic forces of good of which the Archangel Mikhaël is the symbol. Yes, for the Archangel Mikhaël is a real entity and it is he who will be at the head of the egregor formed by all the great Masters and disciples of the Universal White Brotherhood. And, when I speak of the 'disciples of the Universal White Brotherhood' I mean all those who work for the light whatever religion or spiritual fellowship they may belong to.

When the time comes, the Archangel Mikhaël will rise up and, with the help of his army of angels of light[1], will conquer the dragon and bring about the victory that human beings have never ceased asking the Creator for. This is why we should ally ourselves with him and ask him to protect us and allow us to work with him in order to strengthen his victory. Light will triumph over darkness: this has been foretold and it will be so. Why not have a share in that triumph by dedicating your energies to light, goodness and brotherhood every day?

[1] See *Complete Works*, vol. 15, chap. 27, 'Our only weapons: love and light'.

Chapter Twelve

THE DRAGON SPEWS WATER AT THE WOMAN

'Now when the dragon saw that he had been cast to the earth, he persecuted the woman who gave birth to the male child. But the woman was given two wings of a great eagle, that she might fly into the wilderness to her place, where she is nourished for a time and times and half a time, from the presence of the serpent. So the serpent spewed water out of his mouth like a flood after the woman, that he might cause her to be carried away by the flood. But the earth helped the woman, and the earth opened its mouth and swallowed up the flood which the dragon had spewed out of his mouth.'

Revelations 13, 13-16

The Apocalypse says that the Woman was rescued from the dragon by being given two wings of a great eagle and, as we know, tradition has always seen a symbolic opposition between the dragon or serpent which crawls on the ground and the eagle which flies to great heights in the sky[1].

[1] Symbolically, the scorpion has the same meaning as the serpent or dragon. See *Complete Works*, vol. 11, chap. 19.

In an attempt to capture the Woman, the serpent 'spewed water out of his mouth like a flood after the Woman, that he might cause her to be carried away by the flood'. This flood of water has nothing to do with physical water; it represents the dragon's forces and energies. Water is a symbol of life; the currents of energy flowing through the universe are pictured as water, a fluid that sustains and nourishes life. The dragon is a fallen creature, that is true, but, like every other creature, it still possesses life and the flood of water spewed from its mouth is the expression of that life. Whether pure or polluted, water always represents life, and whether that life be divine or angelic, human or demonic, it is still life.

The image that can best help us to understand this idea is that of a river. A river flows sometimes for thousands of miles from a source high up in the mountains until it reaches the sea. The water that bubbles out of a spring is crystal clear, delicious and nourishing but, little by little, as it descends into the plain, it flows through different regions, picking up all the dirt and pollutants of those regions on the way. By the time it reaches the sea, therefore, it has become a liquid that is fit only to water your garden and provide a breeding ground for all kinds of micro-organisms.

In the same way, the river of life gushes, pure and sparkling, from the throne of God and flows down through all the regions of the universe nourishing and watering their inhabitants: the

Seraphim, the Cherubim, the Thrones, Dominations, Powers, Virtues, Principalities, Archangels, Angels and Ishim or Beatified Souls (the Prophets, great Masters and Initiates). But when this powerful torrent descends even lower and reaches the region of ordinary human beings, exactly the same thing happens as with a river on earth that descends from the mountains to the plains and is polluted by the human beings that live along its banks.

On the mental and astral planes, just as on the physical plane, human beings unwittingly pollute this great river of life until it is no better than a swamp of stagnant water made filthy by all that people throw into it, all the emanations of their lower instincts, all their spite and resentment, all their unbridled lust and greed. And we are all obliged to swallow this filthy, contaminated water. But, whether pure or polluted, the life that comes from God is still life, even when it descends into the subterranean regions to nourish their inhabitants. If the entities that we call demons did not have this water of life to drink, how could they continue to exist?

The two opposite ends of the river, the source up in the mountains and the mouth down on the sea coast, represent the two poles of the psychic life: the superconscious and the subconscious, Heaven and Hell. For the ocean has traditionally been given many different symbolic meanings and, because of its unorganized, chaotic nature and its unplumbed depths, one of the things it symbolizes is the birthplace and feeding ground of the forces of darkness, of such malevolent entities, for instance, as the Leviathan, the sea monster mentioned in the Book of Job[2].

The water spewed out by the dragon, therefore, represents some of the forces he expends in his attempt to capture the Woman. It is water, it is life, but it is the lowest level of life. And - and this is also symbolic - that water is swallowed up by the earth. As you know, on the physical plane, the four elements can either reinforce or neutralize each other's action and this is equally true on the psychic plane: the earth can absorb negative currents on the psychic plane as well. This is why I have given you exercises to do with the earth. When you feel upset, beset by negative forces, you can lie down on the ground, make a little hole in the soil for your finger and ask the entities that work there to deliver you from these negative forces[3].

The earth came to the rescue of the Woman by swallowing up the flood spewed out by the dragon; in the same way the earth can help us by absorbing the noxious currents that our lower nature spews over us - for it is this, our lower nature, that is the real dragon. Social development is such that human beings have less and less contact with the earth and

[2] Job 41, 1-10.

[3] See 'The River of Life' in *Complete Works*, vol. 7.

that is a pity, because this contact is always beneficial to the human psyche. I have often advised people suffering from psychosis and obsessions to work the soil, for digging, weeding and planting can be extremely therapeutic. So, as you can see, the symbols of the Apocalypse do have some connection with the problems of everyday life.

Chapter Thirteen

THE BEAST FROM THE SEA AND THE BEAST FROM THE LAND

‘And I saw a beast rising up out of the sea, having seven heads and ten horns, and on his horns ten crowns, and on his heads a blasphemous name. Now the beast which I saw was like a leopard, his feet were like the feet of a bear, and his mouth like the mouth of a lion. And the dragon gave him his power, his throne, and great authority. I saw one of his heads as if it had been mortally wounded, and his deadly wound was healed. And all the world marvelled and followed the beast. So they worshipped the dragon who gave authority to the beast; and they worshipped the beast, saying, “Who is like the beast? Who is able to make war with him?” And he was given a mouth speaking great things and blasphemies, and he was given authority to continue for forty-two months. Then he opened his mouth in blasphemy against God, to blaspheme His name, His tabernacle, and those who dwell in heaven.’

Revelations 13, 1-6.

‘Then I saw another beast coming up out of the

earth, and he had two horns like a lamb and spoke like a dragon. And he exercises all the authority of the first beast in his presence, and causes the earth and those who dwell in it to worship the first beast, whose deadly wound was healed. He performs great signs, so that he even makes fire come down from heaven on the earth in the sight of men. And he deceives those who dwell on the earth by those signs which he was granted to do in the sight of the beast, telling those who dwell on the earth to make an image to the beast who was wounded by the sword and lived … Let him who has understanding calculate the number of the beast, for it is the number of a man: His number is 666.'

Revelations 13, 11-18.

When the dragon was vanquished by the Archangel Mikhaël and his cohorts he was cast down to earth and to the sea: 'Woe to the inhabitants of the earth and the sea! For the devil has come down to you, having great wrath, because he knows that he has a short time'[1]. And on earth his power is reinforced by the two beasts that rise, one from the sea and the other from the earth, for the sea and the earth symbolize a region that has not yet been visited and organized by the spirit, that is to say, the region of man's lower nature[2].

[1] Revelations 12, 12.

[2] See *Complete Works*, vol. 2, chap. 2.

Initiatic Science teaches that there is a cosmic entity of evil known variously as Satan, Lucifer, the Dragon, etc., and that there is also a reservoir of dark, evil forces formed by the accumulation of the evil thoughts, feelings and actions of human beings. These reservoirs are known as 'egregors'. Of course, just as there are egregors of darkness, there are also egregors of light formed by the good thoughts, feelings and actions of human beings. Clairvoyants who have seen the egregors of evil describe them as having the form of ferocious beasts. The beasts that rise from the sea and the earth are the egregors of evil. The dragon gives his power to these beasts and they, in turn, reinforce the power of the dragon by persuading the inhabitants of the earth to worship him and to blaspheme against the name of God.

St John says that the number of the beast that came out of the earth is 666, and this number has given rise to all kinds of interpretations. So many commentators, instead of trying to understand the symbolism of this number, tried anxiously to identify the historical character, doctrine or ideology it represented. The suppositions have varied, of course, with the centuries and, at different times, 666 has been taken to represent Nero, Protestantism, Napoleon, Hitler, Communism, etc. But, in reality, this number is a symbol: three times six, the number six in the three worlds.

The only way to understand the number six is to study it in relation to the number five. Five is the number of man with outstretched arms and legs, man as represented by the five-pointed star, the pentagram. Five represents the man that has freed himself from his animal nature which is symbolized by a tail. Six, therefore, is the number of the animal. You can see from this how important it is for a disciple to work at establishing the Five within himself. How can he do this? By practising the five virtues: wisdom, love, truth, kindness and righteousness.

Figure 6

To advance from animal to man, therefore, is to go from Six to Five. And this is not easy: human nature is still so close to its animal nature, with all its instincts and appetites. We all carry our animal past with us, some in the form of craftiness or treachery, some in the form of brutality, cruelty, gluttony or sensuality, etc. The question, now, is to work to develop the psychic and spiritual qualities we need in order to hold our own against these instinctive tendencies. This is the problem we all have to tackle.

Of course, our animal nature is very powerful because it has existed for a very long time and has had thousands of years in which to practise and become strong through its struggle to survive in very difficult conditions. Look at animals and all the difficulties they have to surmount in order to survive, find food, build a nest or find a lair, defend their territory, raise their young and protect them from predators. How can you expect that instinctive nature to be gentle, kind and merciful when it has had to survive in such conditions? No, but what we also have to remember is that this nature is not the final phase of human development; that it is now time for wisdom and intelligence to come to the fore and offset this great force that we all possess and which Revelations refers to as the Beast. Where must we look in order to find the Beast? In others? No; in ourselves. The Beast is in each one of us. It also exists externally, collectively, that is true, but we can only fully comprehend it if we realize that it is within us; that it is our own lower nature.

So there you are: you must be aware of the extreme importance of the work you are called to do on your lower nature with the weapons of the intellect, the soul and the spirit. Do you imagine that, if you fail to do that work, the Beast is going to be grateful to you for feeding and serving it? Don't you believe it: it will end by devouring you! Remember what St John says about the Great Harlot who sat on the beast with ten horns and seven heads: 'The ten horns (which, as I have told you, symbolize the ten dark Sephiroth) which you saw on the beast, these will hate the harlot, make her desolate and naked, eat her flesh and burn her with fire[3]. Yes, he who is not vigilant will inevitably end by being torn to shreds and devoured by the lower nature that he has always cherished, warmed and nourished so devotedly!

Chapter Fourteen

THE WEDDING FEAST OF THE LAMB

'And I heard, as it were, the voice of a great multitude, as the sound of many waters and as the sound of mighty thunderings, saying, "Alleluia! for the Lord God Omnipotent reigns! Let us be glad and rejoice and give Him glory, for the marriage of the Lamb has come, and His wife has made herself ready'. And to her it was granted to be arrayed in fine linen, clean and bright, for the fine linen is the righteous acts of the saints. Then he said to me, "Write, Blessed are those who are called to the marriage supper of the Lamb!"'

Revelations 19, 6-9.

'Then I, John, saw the holy city, New Jerusalem, coming down out of heaven from God, prepared as a bride adorned for her husband.'

Revelations 21, 2.

'Then one of the seven angels who had the seven bowls filled with the seven last plagues came to me and talked with me, saying, "Come, I will show you the bride, the Lamb's wife". And he carried me away in the spirit to a great and high mountain, and showed me the great city, the holy Jerusalem, descending out of heaven from God, having the glory of God.

Revelations 21, 9-11

A great celebration is being prepared in Heaven, the celebration of the marriage of the Lamb. And the Lamb's spouse is the New Jerusalem. Of course, most people will be very surprised to read that the spouse is a city; they are unprepared to envisage things in this way, for their conception and practice of marriage is so far removed from the deeper reality of marriage. True marriage is the union of the two great cosmic principles, the eternal masculine and feminine principles, which are the origin and cause of all that exists in the universe.

Yes, marriage, true marriage as it is understood by the greatest Initiates, is the union of these two great principles, masculine and feminine, spirit and matter, and this union is a work of the spirit on matter and its fruit is perfect life. Matter is opaque, inert, formless and the spirit unites with it in order to bring it to life and make it luminous and expressive. The spirit is so subtle and elusive that it needs to be joined to something material in order to condense and become concrete. When the spirit succeeds in rendering matter subtler and matter succeeds in condensing the spirit, then they achieve the most extraordinary union, a true fusion. That is what true marriage is.

The Lamb, whose wedding feast is being celebrated, is a symbol of Christ, the Spirit, and his spouse is this earthly city, the symbol of matter, which, through union with him, becomes the Heavenly Jerusalem, the City of God. And just as we celebrate our weddings here on earth with a banquet at which the guests wear their most beautiful clothes, on the spiritual plane also, a wedding is accompanied symbolically by a banquet at which all the guests wear their best ceremonial dress. For a disciple, this wedding feast can take place every day, for the marriage of spirit and matter, of Heaven and earth, takes place every day. Every day, human beings can be united to the divine world thanks to the luminous garment of their aura[1].

Be on your guard, therefore, and make sure that you are there, ready to take part in the banquet to which the Lord, the Divine Mother and all the Heavenly hierarchies invite you. Do you imagine that you will be admitted to this banquet just because you want to be? Oh no; certain conditions have to be fulfilled before they will let you in. If you arrive just like that without having prepared yourself for it, you will meet with the same fate as the man in Jesus' parable who was cast into outer darkness because he had appeared at the wedding party without a

[1] See *Complete Works*, vol. 6, chap. 12, 'The Aura'.

wedding garment[2]. The wedding garment symbolizes a person's inner qualities, the inner state that each one has to develop before he can be admitted to the wedding feast of the Lamb.

Of course, you may never be invited to sit at the head table, at the right hand of the Master of the house but, even if you are in the humblest place at the lower end of the table that doesn't matter; what counts is to be allowed in so that you can participate in the feast.

Chapter Fifteen

THE DRAGON IS BOUND FOR A THOUSAND YEARS

'Then I saw an angel coming down from heaven, having the key to the bottomless pit and a great chain in his hand. He laid hold of the dragon, that serpent of old, who is the Devil and Satan, and bound him for a thousand years; and he cast him into the bottomless pit, and shut him up, and set a seal on him, so that he should deceive the nations no more till the thousand years were finished. But after these things he must be released for a little while.'

Revelations 20, 1-3

So the Dragon has been struck down by the Archangel Mikhaël and the Heavenly hosts and now finds himself chained and cast into the bottomless pit for a thousand years. Later, he will be allowed out again for a little while. What does this mean? Does it mean that evil will reign once again on earth? No, because during the thousand years that the Dragon is chained in the pit, he will not simply be left to his own devices: something will be done about him. He will be groomed and reformed; he will have teachers who will put him through a gruelling apprenticeship;

there will even be chiropodists, manicurists and dentists to file his teeth and claws, to remove his venom and render him inoffensive! Yes, why not? There are all kinds of underground workshops in which he will be given special treatments to clean him up a bit. Otherwise, what would be the point of keeping a dragon shut up for a thousand years? When he was released he would only create the same devastation and the same damage as before. You cannot rehabilitate a dragon if you don't treat him a bit roughly. This is why some highly skilled educators will be given the task of taking care of him. They will tell him, 'Aha, now it's your turn: you have tormented human beings for long enough so now you are going to be taught a lesson!'

It is contrary to divine wisdom to kill creatures or to allow them to remain inactive. Cosmic Intelligence tolerates neither sloth nor death and this is why it is pre-ordained that, one day, even the most depraved and vicious creatures, the Dragon and demons, will be allowed to return to God. Don't you believe me? It is quite true. Human beings are so cruel, they don't even want the devils to reform; they think that they should burn in Hell for all eternity! No, no; the Lord intends to reform them and bring them back to Himself but, as He is infinitely patient, He is in no great hurry, so the devils are still there to torment human beings. The time will come, however, when they will all be bound and unable to torment human beings any longer. And that time is getting near.

You will be wondering how I know all this. I know it because I have read it, of course. Where? Ah, certainly not in books written by human beings. I don't trust the books of human beings any longer; they contain too many errors, too much nonsense; I don't waste my time reading them. The only book I read now is the Book of Living Nature. It is in this Book that I have discovered that God's love and life reach down into the depths of the earth, even into the bottomless pit. Yes, even there, there are still some particles of life which make it possible for the creatures of those regions to survive. And if the life of God reaches even to such depths why should those creatures not be allowed to survive?

The Dragon will not be killed, therefore, nor will he simply be left as he is: he will be re-educated. Unless, of course, he is eaten! Yes, if you study the Talmud you will read that in the depths of the oceans lives a monster known as Leviathan, the symbol of evil, and that, on the last day, Leviathan will be caught and cut up and his flesh will be salted and preserved for the enjoyment of the righteous. You must try to understand. In any case, this is what the Talmud says, so you can imagine the marvellous feasts that are in store for the righteous; all that delicious meat and all the jollifications to look forward to! If we were to take all this quite literally, of course, most people would be completely disgusted. As I say: you have to understand; it has to be interpreted. And how should it be interpreted? Well, since Leviathan, who is a monster, is destined to be turned into a choice morsel for the pleasure of the righteous, it means that if we know how to make use of evil, it can become a nourishment, that is to say, a source of enrichment and blessings.

It is quite clear, therefore, that evil can be tamed, chloroformed and put to good use; we can even cut it up and eat it, but we cannot kill it. So wouldn't it be much better to learn to use it? This is a new understanding of the symbol of the Dragon.

Chapter Sixteen

THE NEW HEAVEN AND THE NEW EARTH

‘And I saw a new heaven and a new earth, for the first heaven and the first earth had passed away.’

Revelations 21, 1

Why a new heaven and a new earth? If we take this passage literally we have to wonder whether God has to begin His creation all over again and why. Have the first heaven and the first earth become obsolete? It might be conceivable that the earth should get old, for it is, after all, made of materials which wear out and are subject to rust and, with time, it might have to be replaced. But heaven is supposed to be made of absolutely pure, luminous, incorruptible, eternal materials; how could it possibly wear out? Also, Genesis tells us that when the Lord created heaven and earth He looked at them and ‘saw that they were good’; how could He now find that the earth He had created was not so good after all, and that He was going to have to make another one? This does not say much for the perfection of God! Besides, where would all the inhabitants of the universe, the myriads of Angels and Archangels, live while the renovations are going on? What a commotion and what a lot of problems for the Lord! Well, all that is obviously absurd so we have to interpret this text differently.

We have to understand that the word 'heaven' means one thing and the word 'earth' means something else. In the language of symbols, heaven represents the spiritual dimension of man, the realm of thought and concepts, whereas the earth represents the realm of materialization, of physical realizations. Just as the heaven and earth of the cosmos form a unit, so the heaven and earth of man are also one. A 'new heaven' means new ideas, a new perception and understanding, a new philosophy which necessarily leads to a 'new earth', that is to say, to new attitudes, a new way of doing things and a new way of living. Our heads are in heaven and our feet are on earth. The feet walk in the direction indicated by the head; they go where the head leads them, into terrain that the head has already explored. In other words, man's behaviour, the things he does and the way he does them, will change in line with the changed head, that is to say, the new philosophy.

But is this new heaven that God is busy creating really new? No, not really: it has been there for all eternity, but to human beings, it will be new. It has always been there but they have never seen it, so when they discover it, all of a sudden, it will be new to them.

A new heaven and a new earth ...actually, we don't even know what the word 'new' means. Look at any river: the Seine, the Danube or the Thames; the name remains the same but isn't the water that flows in it always new? And the same is true of the sun: the sun is the same every day and yet its emanations and radiations are different at each instant. What is new, therefore, is life, the content. If you are capable of going far enough and high enough and reaching beyond the container to the content, to life itself, then you will see that everything in heaven and earth is always new.

A new heaven and a new earth, therefore, means that the consciousness of human beings will rise to a level on which invisible realities that have always existed will at last become visible to them. The sun has always been there but most human beings are not aware of it. As long as they never rejoice in the sun, as long as they never contemplate it and sense that it is a living, intelligent being, as long as they never feel the desire to resemble it, it means that they have still not discovered it, that they are still in the mouldy, wormeaten, obsolete heaven of the past.

Now you must not imagine that you have to wait for some great cosmic upheaval before you can become aware of this new heaven: you can be a part of it already, today. Every time you entertain pure thoughts and feelings, every time you decide to work for a high ideal, you are already in the new heaven and this new heaven necessarily leads to the new earth, for he who embraces a sublime philosophy is obliged to change his behaviour and his way of doing things. All the methods that you are learning here with regard to nutrition, breathing, work, the creation of children, your relations with other human beings and with the universe ...all this is the new earth. Why don't you enter it? What are you waiting for?

Unfortunately, it seems that there are not too many candidates and that it is going to be the story of the cattle and their new stable all over again. Let me tell you this story: two brothers had inherited their father's farm and were dividing the livestock between them. When it came to dividing the cattle, the younger brother, who was not very bright and often had strange ideas which he thought were very wise, said, 'Let's build a new cattle shed and, when it's finished, we'll let the cattle choose which one they want to go into. Those that go into the old shed will be yours and those that go into the new one will be mine'. Imagine: a referendum for the cattle! Well, as the elder brother had no objection to the plan, the new shed was built and, when it was finished, the cattle were allowed to go to the shed of their choice. Naturally enough, the whole herd did what they had always done and went into the old shed. You can imagine how mortified the younger brother was to see that only one blind old bull chose the new one!

I'm afraid that there is a danger of the same thing happening with the new heaven and the new earth that the Lord is creating. I sometimes feel like asking Him: 'When You decided to create a new heaven and a new earth, Lord, did You know the mentality of human beings? What did You hope for? What did You expect? Look at your new heaven; it's empty: there's no one there!' Yes, I'm like the old, blind bull; I don't know why, but I seem to be the only one to choose the new heaven. Of course, I'm not going to say all that to the Lord; He knows what He is doing. Perhaps He only wants to see how many will enter His new heaven and walk on His new earth. As far as I can see there are not many, and that worries me.

How about you? Are some of you at least going to make the effort to enter the new heaven, that is to say, to accept the new philosophy and put it into practice? And it is precisely this, the putting it into practice, that constitutes the new earth. As you see, all this has to be understood symbolically otherwise none of it makes sense. How could heaven and earth disappear to make room for another heaven and another earth? Heaven will stay as it is and the earth too (unless human beings destroy it themselves), but it is our way of thinking and our way of living that has to change.

In another passage in Revelations we read: 'And behold, there was a great earthquake; and the sun became black as sackcloth of hair, and the moon became like blood. And the stars of heaven fell to the earth, as a fig tree drops its late figs when it is shaken by a mighty wind'[1]. And the Gospels tell us that Jesus prophesied similar events: 'The sun will be darkened, and the moon will not give its light; the stars will fall from heaven'[2]. And yet our poor little planet is so tiny that it doesn't even have room for a star: a single star is thousands of times bigger than the earth! How could anyone imagine that they will all start falling on us at once? The stars don't even know of the existence of this speck of dust that calls itself earth and whose inhabitants spend all their time arguing and quarrelling amongst themselves: why should they suddenly decide to fall on it? No, put your minds at rest: the stars are not going to fall from the heavens. But, symbolically, a great many 'stars' are going to fall: these are the stars that shine with earthly glory and have been put on a pedestal without having done anything to deserve it. With the coming of the new heaven and the new earth these stars are going to lose the rank and renown they enjoy today.

And what about the sun that is going to be darkened? This sun is the philosophy that holds sway in the world, a philosophy that, in alienating itself from true Initiatic Science, has become so exclusively intellectual that it is no longer capable of solving the new problems of life. It is this sun, to which human beings have clung for so long, that is

[1] Revelations 6, 12-14

[2] Matthew 24, 29

going to lose its light.

As for the moon, which represents the realm of religion, it too will lose its brightness. In other words, the official religions, which are built on false foundations, on superstition, prejudice and fanaticism, are going to lose all influence and authority.

The Gospels also say, 'You will see the Son of Man coming on the clouds of Heaven'. This means that Christ will come in the thoughts, in the minds, of men. For clouds, which belong to the realm of air, represent thoughts: their forms, which change ceaselessly under the influence of the winds, are an expression of the mental world. These, then, are the prophecies of Jesus and St John, and the sun, the moon, the stars and the clouds they speak of are not those that we see in the sky: they are symbols of the corresponding realities in our psyche.

So, now, this is all quite clear: you must not wait for the end of the world in the way that Christians have often waited for it. Time and time again we have been told that the end of the world was upon us - even the exact date was prophesied. People panicked and prepared for death but the fatal day came and went and life went on as before. There were, perhaps, a few upheavals here and there, but the world has never come to an end. Only eras have ended. It is important to understand that 'the world', in this case, means an era, and we are constantly living through the last days of one era and the first days of the next one. And today, too, we are living in the last days of the world, for a new era is dawning.

Mankind will never entirely disappear. Don't worry about it: human beings are very tough; they can survive anything! On the other hand, there are certainly going to be all kinds of cataclysms and upheavals; we are truly at the end of an era. This is why you have to get ready to enter the new heaven and to walk on the new earth.

Chapter Seventeen

THE HEAVENLY CITY

‘And he showed me the great city, the holy Jerusalem, descending out of heaven from God, having the glory of God. And her light was like a most precious stone, like a jasper stone, clear as crystal. Also she had a great and high wall with twelve gates, and twelve angels at the gates, and names written on them, which are the names of the twelve tribes of the children of Israel: three gates on the east, three gates on the north, three gates on the south, and three gates on the west. Now the wall of the city had twelve foundations, and on them were the names of the twelve apostles of the Lamb.

And he who talked with me had a gold rod to measure the city, its gates, and its wall. And the city is laid out as a square, and its length is as great as its breadth. And he measured the city with the reed: twelve thousand furlongs. Its length, breadth, and height are equal. Then he measured its wall: one hundred and forty-four cubits, according to the measure of a man, that is, of an angel.

And the construction of its wall was of jasper; and the city was pure gold, like clear glass. And the foundations of the wall of the city were adorned with all kinds of precious stones: the first foundation was jasper, the second sapphire, the third chalcedony, the fourth emerald, the fifth sardonyx, the sixth sardius, the seventh chrysolite, the eighth beryl, the ninth topaz, the tenth chrysoprase, the eleventh jacinth, and the twelfth amethyst. And the twelve gates were twelve pearls: each individual gate was of one pearl. And the street of the city was pure gold, like transparent glass.

But I saw no temple in it, for the Lord God Almighty and the Lamb are its temple. And the city had no need of the sun or of the moon to shine in it, for the glory of God illuminated it, and the Lamb is its light. And the nations of those who are saved shall walk in its light, and the kings of the earth bring their glory and honour into it. Its gates shall not be shut at all by day (there shall be no night there). And they shall bring the glory and the honour of the nations into it. But there shall by no means enter it anything that defiles, or causes an abomination or a lie, but only those who are written in the Lamb's Book of Life.

And he showed me a pure river of water of life, clear as crystal, proceeding from the throne of God and of the Lamb. In the middle of its street, and on either side of the river, was the tree of life, which bore twelve fruits, each tree yielding its fruit every month. And the leaves of the tree were for the healing of the nations. And there shall be no more curse, but the throne of God and of the Lamb will be in it, and His servants shall serve Him. They shall see His face, and His name shall be on their foreheads. And there shall be no night there: they need no lamp nor light of the sun, for the Lord God gives them light. And they shall reign for ever and ever'.

Revelations 21, 10 - 22, 5

I

The Cubic Stone

The city described by St John is a cube: 'Its length, breadth and height are equal'. In the symbolism of the cube, as in that of the square, we have the number four, the number that signifies matter, for matter is the four elements (earth, water, air and fire), the four directions of the compass (north, south, east and west), etc. The cubic form of the New Jerusalem, the Bride of the Lamb, clearly indicates that it is a symbol of the matter with which the Lamb, that is to say, Christ, the spirit, unites and, in uniting with it, gives it the brilliance of a precious stone, the transparency of crystal.

But the symbolism of the cube goes much

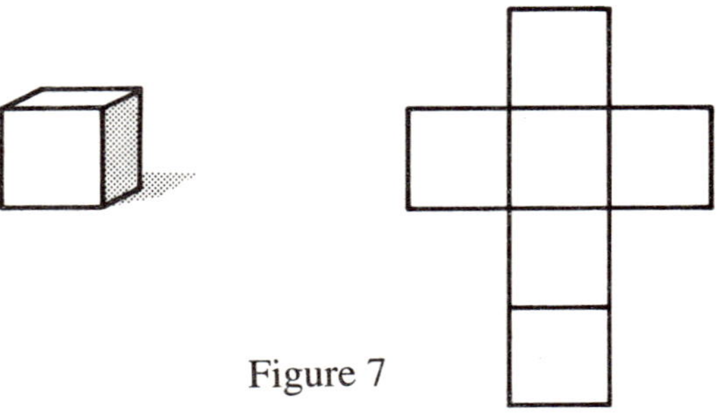

Figure 7

further than this, for the development of a cube produces a cross.

For cabbalists, the three-dimensional cross contains and sums up all the principles of creation.

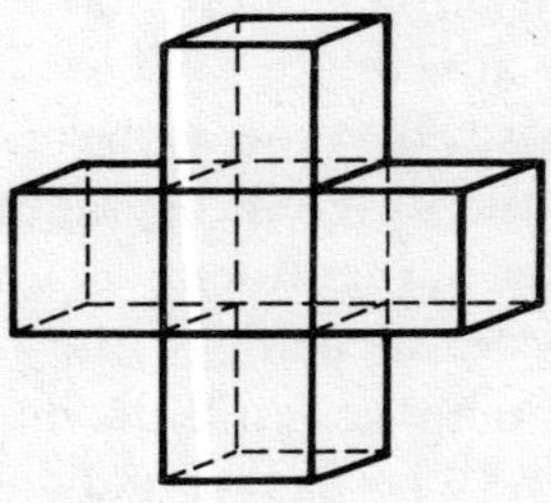

Figure 8

If you count the faces of this figure you will find that there are twenty-two. A letter of the Hebrew alphabet is inscribed on each face and each of these letters corresponds to one of the twenty-two Tarot cards. The cross, therefore, is the symbolic representation of the twenty-two powers with which God created the universe.

Christianity has emphasized the painful, tragic aspect of the cross, its association with death and, specifically, of course, with the death of Jesus. But we must look further for the true significance of the cross, for it is much vaster than that: the cross is matter, the matter that receives and is vivified by the spirit. To be sure, it can happen that the spirit descends into matter and lets itself go to sleep. If it is not strong enough to vivify the matter that receives it, it can be buried, entombed, by it. Unfortunately, this is what happens with a great many people who allow the spirit to be buried within them. Matter is a cross on which the spirit ceaselessly sacrifices itself, but the sacrifice of the spirit has meaning only if matter allows itself to be transformed and become purer and more alive.

For alchemists, the cross is the crucible in which they carry out the different operations designed to transform matter into gold but, as I have often told you, for a true alchemist, the matter to be transformed is in himself: it is the matter of his own being. This is why he has to study all the different elements of which it is composed, the way in which they combine and the formulas that enable him to transmute them.

We have to study all the elements of our cross, our own matter and, just as God worked with the living cross, the Logos, in creating the universe, we have to work with these elements and combine them like the letters of the alphabet to transform our own being into the New Jerusalem. As long as we fail to understand that it is man himself who is the cross and who has to work with that cross, we shall not make much progress on the path of evolution.

So, as you now understand very well, the New Jerusalem is not a city and it is no good thinking that it is going to drop from heaven, as so many Christians have thought in the course of the last two thousand years: the New Jerusalem is the symbol of a human being who has worked with the power of the spirit to transform his own matter. And all the architectural elements described by St John - the foundations of precious stones, the pearly gates, etc. - are also symbolic.

II

The Foundations of Precious Stones

Precious stones are the end result of a tremendous work of transformation carried out by the Intelligence of Nature on the raw material that the earth bears in its womb; it is as though the earth aspired not only to reflect but also to give concrete form to the splendours of Heaven. This is why all religions have considered precious stones to be symbols of the divine virtues and, if they constitute the foundations of the New Jerusalem, it is because the virtues are the true foundations of man's inner life. Precious stones represent the ideal for which we must strive by the transmutation of the raw material of our instincts.

How many men have ever understood the lesson contained in precious stones? The only thing that interests them is to possess them. For thousands of years, hundreds of poor, unfortunate wretches have been forced to work in the most frightful conditions in underground mines to satisfy this craving, while others have cheated, lied, stolen and murdered to obtain the fruits of their labours. All this because a handful of the rich and powerful want to show off their crowns, necklaces, bracelets, rings, tie-pins and cuff-links glittering with diamonds, rubies, emeralds, etc. I'm sorry to say that all that is a very long way from the Heavenly Jerusalem!

There is no law that forbids you to love precious stones or even to want to possess some as long as you have the right attitude towards them. 'And what attitude is that?' you will ask. You should see them as a link, a means of communication with the spiritual world. You should focus your thoughts on them, on their purity, their colours, their capacity to allow light to pass through them, and then ask them to enter you and give you all their properties and virtues so that your whole being may shine with the light of sapphires, diamonds, rubies, emeralds and topazes, and so on. This is why we should value and seek to possess precious stones: not in order to use them as ornaments but in order to be illumined and nourished by their quintessence[1].

[1] See *The Foundations* in chapter 11 of 'The Living Book of Nature', Collection Izvor, No. 216.

III

The Gates of Pearl

The Heavenly City is surrounded by a great and high wall of jasper and the City itself is of pure gold 'like clear glass', which means that it has the transparency and brilliance of light. A wall is a protection; the wall surrounding the Heavenly City is the symbol of a powerful aura that surrounds and protects man, for he who possesses a powerful aura is protected by the radiance of his own light.

The wall is pierced by twelve gates: three to the north, three to the south, three to the east and three to the west, and St John says that each gate consists of a pearl. The twelve gates facing the four cardinal points of the compass are another representation of the twelve signs of the Zodiac: Aries, Taurus, Gemini, etc. and it is through these gates that the currents and forces and invisible entities at work in the universe enter and influence man. On these gates are inscribed the names of the twelve tribes of the children of Israel, and we have already seen their correspondence with the twelve signs of the Zodiac.

But did you know that these twelve gates or openings of the universe also exist in each human being? Where are they? The two eyes, two ears, two nostrils, the mouth, the two breasts and the navel add up to ten … and I think that you can find the last two for yourselves. Just as the gates of the Zodiac serve to give passage to cosmic influences, so the gates of our own physical bodies also give passage to the forces and spirits that enter us, for man is built in such a way as to be capable of communications and exchange with the whole universe.

The Book of Revelations says that the gates of the New Jerusalem are pearls; yes, because a pearl catches and retains light on its lustrous surface and is considered a symbol of purity. For those who have already accomplished a genuine work of inner purification, the gates of their bodies serve to establish communications with the subtle, luminous elements in space. This is why Revelations also says that an Angel stands at each gate, for an Angel is pure energy and that energy both attracts beneficial influences and transforms any negative currents that attempt to infiltrate. Angels guard the doors of all those who have worked to transform their being into the tabernacle of the living God.

A little later, the text says, 'I saw no temple in it, for the Lord God Almighty and the Lamb are its temple. And the city had no need of the sun or of the moon to shine in it, for the glory of God illuminated it, and the Lamb is its light.' A holy city, a pure physical body are, themselves, temples; any other temple is unnecessary. Even the sun and moon are unnecessary, for, as I have already explained, the sun symbolizes the intellect and the moon the heart. Those in whom divine light and love dwell have no more need of the sun or the moon, of philosophy or religion.

'Its gates shall not be shut at all by day for there shall be no night there.' When one is illumined there is no night. Those who are illumined are inhabited by the inner light; even when they are asleep there is no night for them. Of course, for most people, it is sometimes day and sometimes night; at one moment they are illuminated and the next moment they are in darkness. But once true illumination comes, once the Holy Spirit illumines them, nothing can darken them again.

The names of those who have attained this level of spiritual life are inscribed in the Book of the Lamb. Here, on earth, you may be a member of a Church or a spiritual confraternity but that does not necessarily mean that you will be accepted in the world above, for the earth is, as it were, no more than an antechamber; it is not the Holy of Holies. It is much more difficult to gain acceptance on high; it takes years of striving and hard work but once you are accepted your name is inscribed in the register and you receive the help and gifts you need from Heaven, every day. It is exactly like being registered as a government employee: you receive a salary and allowances, bonuses, etc.

Jesus said, 'Behold, I give you the authority to

trample on serpents and scorpions, and over all the power of the enemy, and nothing shall by any means hurt you. Nevertheless, do not rejoice in this, that the spirits are subject to you, but rather rejoice because your names are written in Heaven'[2]. Once your name is written in the Book of Life Heaven will never forget you; It will always send you strength, health and joy. You will always feel yourself supported, counselled and guided and, if there are trials and difficulties that have to be faced up to and endured, whether they will not last so long or you will be given the fortitude to endure them.

So there you have the true Scriptures, the Living Scriptures. all you have to do now is to make the efforts and sacrifices that will allow you to enter the gates of the Heavenly Jerusalem, for this is the goal and, once you are there, you will be safe[3]!

[2] Luke 10, 19-20

[3] See also *The Gates* in 'The Living Book of Nature', Collection Izvor, No. 216.

IV

The River of Life

The city of pure gold, with its walls of jasper, its gates of pearl and its foundations of precious stones, has a river flowing through it, 'a pure river of water of life, clear as crystal, proceeding from the throne of God and of the Lamb'. Yes, because life is a flowing, a circulation, a decanting of energies, and the river of life that gushes from the Divine Source flows downwards and irrigates every region of the universe.

According to cabbalistic Science, this river flows, first of all, into the first Sephirah, Kether. As Kether is filled and overflows, its waters pour into the following Sephirah, Chokmah. Chokmah, in turn, is filled and overflows and its waters pour into Binah. When Binah is full, its waters overflow into Chesed, and so on: from Chesed to Geburah, from Geburah to Tiphareth, from Tiphareth to Netzach, from Netzach to Hod and from Hod to Yesod the waters of life flow down to Malkuth, the earth. The Sephiroth are sacred vessels that are constantly filled by the inexhaustible source of life.

It was this river that St John saw in his vision: 'In

the middle of its street, and on either side of the river, was the tree of life, which bore twelve fruits, each tree yielding its fruit every month. And the leaves of the tree were for the healing of the nations'. To be sure, this is a very strange tree: how can it be planted on both banks of the river and yield fruit every month? In order to understand these two symbols of the tree and the river, we have to remember, once again, that the City is an image of a human being.

We read that a river flows through the centre of the City and that on its banks is a tree that yields fruit every month: this centre is the solar plexus. The solar plexus is part of the sympathetic nervous system which I have often spoken about and which we have studied from the point of view of Initiatic Science. The sympathetic nervous system consists of a series of centres running from the brain to the base of the spinal cord with a peripheral system of nerves and ganglia joined to each other by a network of nerve fibres known as plexuses. The solar plexus, which is on the level of the stomach, is one of these.

The sympathetic nervous system

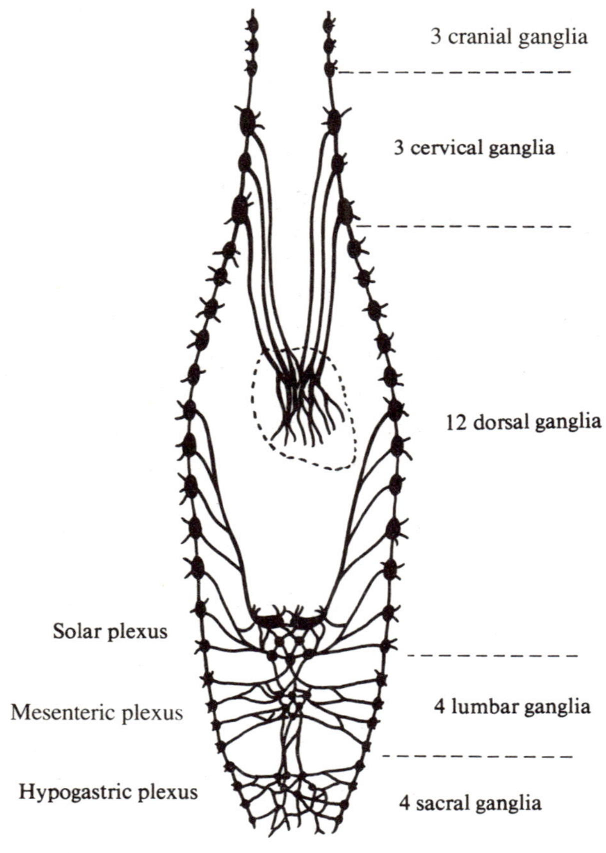

Figure 9

This figure shows the path followed by the current of energy (the river) that flows from the brain (Heaven, the divine world), down the length of the spine and, through the intermediary of the twelve pairs of dorsal nerves and ganglia (the roots of the tree), irrigates the solar plexus (the Tree of Life that grows in the centre of the City). And if this tree produces fruit in each of the twelve months of the year, it is because it too is related to the Zodiac, each sign of which possesses its own specific properties.

Adam and Eve tasted the fruits of the Tree of the Knowledge of Good and Evil in the Garden of Eden and became subject to sickness and death. The fruits of the Tree of Life, which represent the qualities and virtues of the constellations of the Zodiac, are designed, on the contrary, to heal the nations. These, therefore, are the fruits that we must eat. In the order in which they occur in the Zodiac, these are: Aries, activity; Taurus, sensitivity and kindness; Gemini, a taste for study; Cancer, the perception of the invisible world; Leo, nobility and courage; Virgo, purity; Libra, a sense of cosmic equilibrium; Scorpio, the understanding of life and death; Sagittarius, the bond with Heaven; Capricorn, the domination of self and of others; Aquarius, brotherhood and universality, and Pisces, sacrifice. These are the qualities of the fruits of the Tree of Life. And St John tells us that even the leaves of the Tree served to heal the nations. It is not only the fruits of the Tree that possess beneficial properties, therefore, but even its leaves, flowers and roots. There is no part of the Tree of Life that is not useful: its elements are all beneficial and all capable of working miracles.

In the Heavenly City - that is, in the new man inspired by the new Teaching - these two images, the river and the tree, represent love and wisdom. The river is love and the tree growing from its two banks is wisdom, for wisdom has two banks and love, which is one, flows between them. Wisdom is on the outside; it embraces; it is the container, whereas love is on the inside, it is the content. This is why the tree straddles the river. The tree and the river are both in the city and, as love and wisdom, they are both in every human being who studies and applies the true Teaching. The New Jerusalem cannot exist unless the river (love) and the tree (wisdom) both exist. When love and wisdom reign it will be the Kingdom of God and there will be no more night, because the light will shine in every being.

V

The Coming of the New Jerusalem

The New Jerusalem, as we have seen, is the paradigm of the perfect life. This is what I have been talking to you about for years, even if I have not always mentioned it specifically for fear of provoking a reaction of impatience: 'Oh, why this constant reference to the Jewish religion?' But how can anyone fail to see that, by the beauty and wealth of its symbolism, the vision described by St John expresses more eloquently than any other the higher life to which we must aspire. In its proportions, its measurements and the elements of which it is composed, the New Jerusalem is a reflection of the cosmic order. It is this order that must be brought down to earth and it is we who have to bring it, for it will not happen otherwise. The Kingdom of God can be established on earth but we must not imagine that a city is going to drop from Heaven just like that, all by itself. If St John says that it will come down from Heaven, it is because, symbolically, light - that is to say the intelligence and wisdom that make it possible to organize and harmonize things - always comes from above, from Heaven, to be realized, materialized on earth.

In reality, therefore, the New Jerusalem is the symbol of the spiritual work that each human being must accomplish within himself. When each one of us has done this work the New Jerusalem will descend into the collective body of mankind. It is coming; it has been on its way for a long time now, but it needs a great deal of time to become flesh and blood. Day and night, the spirits of light are at work on human beings, cleansing them of all their dark, discordant particles and replacing them with other purer, more luminous particles that vibrate in harmony with Heaven. Thousands of new Jerusalems are being prepared to join in forming the one New Jerusalem in which all human beings will live in brotherhood and peace. And it is in your best interest to work to become that New Jerusalem for, even if it does not become incarnate in the world in the form of an ideal society, you can still enjoy its blessings in your own being. Two thousand years ago, Christ said, 'I am coming!' Was he deceiving us? No; all his predictions have been accomplished. He has already come into the hearts and souls of some. He is in the process of coming for others and, in the future, He will come for the whole of humanity.

The New Jerusalem, therefore, is, first and foremost, man himself. Secondly, it is the ideal society and, ultimately, it is the true universal Church of God, the Church of the Spirit and of Truth, the Church of all the great Initiates. No one can prevent this Church from coming and, when it comes, all these things will be explained, everything will become clear, for Scripture tells us that God will dwell in men and write His Law in their hearts. When this day comes, men will not need anyone to preach religion or morals to them; they will all know inwardly what to do, how to love, how to serve and how to work. For centuries, Christians have dreamed of this glorious City and longed for it to come down from Heaven. How can they be made to understand, now, that it is they themselves that are the New Jerusalem? To be sure, as things are today, they are still in the old Jerusalem, still in the grip of disorder and discord, but it is within their grasp to become that City of pure gold whose foundations of precious stones are the virtues (and the spiritual life can have no foundations more solid than the virtues) and whose pearly gates ensure the subtlest intercourse with the luminous entities of the universe.

The New Jerusalem is the perfect man, the perfect social life, the Kingdom of peace and righteousness in which reigns Melchizedek, king of Salem. Yes, this Kingdom truly exists and has always existed. It is thanks to its continued existence that the authentic tradition has survived, for it is from this Initiatic centre that all the great Masters have come to bring light to mankind.

Try, now, to keep this image of the New Jerusalem alive within you, for it is this that will nourish, strengthen and enlighten you. Human beings need powerful, luminous images of this nature that work on them and urge them forward on the path of evolution.

By the same author

Izvor Collection

TABLE OF CONTENTS

206 – A PHILOSOPHY OF UNIVERSALITY

1. What is a Sect ? – 2. No Church is Eternal – 3. The Spirit Behind the Form – 4. The Advent of the Church of St. John – 5. The Foundations of a Universal Religion – 6. The Great Universal White Brotherhood – 7. For a Universal Notion of the Family – 8. Brotherhood, a Higher State of Consciousness – 9. The Annual Conventions at the Bonfin – 10. The Universal Dimension of All Our Activities.

207 – WHAT IS A SPIRITUAL MASTER ?

1. How to Recognize a True Spiritual Master – 2. The Necessity for a Spiritual Master – 3. The Sorcerer's Apprentice – 4. The Exotic Should not be Confused with Spirituality – 5. Learn How to Balance the Material and Spiritual Worlds – 6. A Master is a Mirror Reflecting the Truth – 7. A Master is There Only to Give Light – 8. The Disciple and His Master – 9. The Universal Dimension of a Master – 10. The Magical Presence of a Master – 11. Identification – 12. 'Except Ye Become as Little Children...'

208 – THE EGREGOR OF THE DOVE OR THE REIGN OF PEACE

1. Towards a Better Understanding of Peace – 2. The Advantages of Unity amongst Nations – 3. Aristocracy and Democracy – 4. About Money – 5. The Distribution of Wealth – 6. Communism and Capitalism – 7. Towards a New Understanding of Economics – 8. What Every Politician Should Know – 9. The Kingdom of God.

209 – CHRISTMAS AND EASTER IN THE INITIATIC TRADITION

1. The Feast of the Nativity – 2. The Second Birth – 3. Birth on the Different Planes of Being – 4. 'Except Ye Die Ye Shall not Live' – 5. The Resurrection and the Last Judgment – 6. The Body of Glory.

210 – THE TREE OF THE KNOWLEDGE OF GOOD AND EVIL

1. The Serpent of Genesis – 2. What Good is Evil ? – 3. Beyond Good and Evil – 4. Until the Harvest – 5. The Philosophy of Unity – 6. Into the Wilderness to Be Tempted – 7. The Undesirables – 8. Suicide is not the Answer – 9. The Real Weapons – 10. The Science of the Initiates, or the Inner Lamps.

211 – FREEDOM, THE SPIRIT TRIUMPHANT

1. Man's Psychic Structure – 2. Mind over Matter – 3. Fate and Freedom – 4. Freedom through Death – 5. Sharing in the Freedom of God – 6. True Freedom : a Consecration of Self – 7. Freedom through Self-Limitation – 8. Anarchy and Freedom – 9. The Notion of Hierarchy – 10. The Synarchy Within.

212 – LIGHT IS A LIVING SPIRIT

1. Light : Essence of Creation – 2. The Sun's Rays, their Nature and Activity – 3. Gold is Condensed Sunlight – 4. Light Enables us to See and be Seen – 5. Working with Light – 6. The Prism : a Symbol of Man – 7. Purity Clears the Way for Light – 8. Living with the Intensity of Light – 9. The Spiritual Laser.

213 – MAN'S TWO NATURES, HUMAN AND DIVINE

1. Human Nature or Animal Nature ? – 2.The Lower Self is a Reflection – 3. Man's True Identity – 4. Methods of Escape – 5. The Sun Symbolizes the Divine Nature – 6. Put the Personality to Work – 7. Perfection Comes with the Higher Self – 8. The Silent Voice of the Higher Self – 9. Only by Serving the Divine Nature – 10. Address the Higher Self in Others – 11. Man's Return to God, the Victory.

214 – HOPE FOR THE WORLD : SPIRITUAL GALVANOPLASTY

1. What is Spiritual Galvanoplasty ? – 2. Reflections of the Two Principles – 3. Marriages Made in Heaven – 4. Love Freely Given – 5. Love on the Lower Plane – 6. Love on the Higher Plane – 7. Love's Goal is Light – 8. The Solar Nature of Sexual Energy – 9. Mankind Transformed – 10. The Original Experiment and the New One – 11. Replenish the Earth ! – 12. Woman's place – 13. The Cosmic Child.

215 – THE TRUE MEANING OF CHRIST'S TEACHING

1. 'Our Father Which Art in Heaven' – 2. 'My Father and I Are One' – 3. 'Be Ye Perfect, Even as Your Father Who is in Heaven is Perfect' – 4. 'Seek Ye First the Kingdom of God and His Justice' – 5. 'On Earth as it is in Heaven' – 6. 'He That Eateth My Flesh and Drinketh My Blood Hath Eternal Life' – 7. 'Father, Forgive Them, For They Know Not What They Do' – 8. 'Unto Him that Smiteth Thee on the One Cheek...' – 9. 'Watch and Pray'.

216 – THE LIVING BOOK OF NATURE

1. The Living Book of Nature – 2. Day and Night – 3. Spring Water or Stagnant Water – 4. Marriage, a Universal Symbol – 5. Distilling

the Quintessence – 6. The Power of Fire – 7. The Naked Truth – 8. Building a House – 9. Red and White – 10. The River of Life – 11. The New Jerusalem – Perfect Man. I – The Gates. II – The Foundations – 12. Learning to Read and Write.

217 – NEW LIGHT ON THE GOSPELS

1. 'Men do not Put New Wine into Old Bottles' – 2. 'Except Ye Become as Little Children' – 3. The Unjust Stewart – 4. 'Lay up for Yourselves Treasures in Heaven' – 5. The Strait Gate – 6. 'Let Him Which is on the Housetop not Come Down...' – 7. The Calming of the Storm – 8. The First Shall Be Last – 9. The Parable of the Five Wise and the Five Foolish Virgins – 10. 'This is Life Eternal, that they Might Know Thee the Only True God'.

218 – THE SYMBOLIC LANGUAGE OF GEOMETRICAL FIGURES

1. Geometrical Symbolism – 2. The Circle – 3. The Triangle – 4. The Pentagram – 5. The Pyramid – 6. The Cross – 7. The Quadrature of the Circle.

219 – MAN'S SUBTLE BODIES AND CENTRES
the Aura, the Solar Plexus, the Chakras...

1. Human Evolution and the Development of the Spiritual Organs – 2. The Aura – 3. The Solar Plexus – 4. The Hara Centre – 5. Kundalini Force – 6. The Chakras: The Chakra System I. – The Chakra System II. Ajna and Sahasrara.

220 – THE ZODIAC, KEY TO MAN AND TO THE UNIVERSE

1. The Enclosure of the Zodiac – 2. The Zodiac and the Forming of Man – 3. The Planetary Cycle of Hours and Days – 4. The Cross of Destiny – 5. The Axes of Aries-Libra and Taurus-Scorpio – 6. The Virgo-Pisces Axis – 7. The Leo-Aquarius Axis – 8. The Fire and Water Triangles – 9. The Philosophers' Stone : the Sun, the Moon and Mercury – 10. The Twelve Tribes of Israel and the Twelve Labours of Hercules in Relation to the Zodiac.

221 – TRUE ALCHEMY OR THE QUEST FOR PERFECTION

1. Spiritual Alchemy – 2. The Human Tree – 3. Character and Temperament – 4. Our Heritage from the Animal Kingdom – 5. Fear – 6. Stereotypes – 7. Grafting – 8. The Use of Energy – 9. Sacrifice,

the Transmutation of Matter – 10. Vainglory and Divine Glory – 11. Pride and Humility – 12. The Sublimation of Sexual Energy.

222 – MAN'S PSYCHIC LIFE: ELEMENTS AND STRUCTURES

1. Know Thyself – 2. The Synoptic Table – 3. Several Souls and Several Bodies – 4. Heart, Mind, Soul and Spirit – 5. The Apprenticeship of the Will – 6. Body, Soul and Spirit – 7. Outer Knowledge and Inner Knowledge – 8. From Intellect to Intelligence – 9. True Illumination – 10. The Causal Body – 11. Consciousness – 12. The Subconscious – 13. The Higher Self.

223 – CREATION: ARTISTIC AND SPIRITUAL

1. Art, Science and Religion – 2. The Divine Sources of Inspiration – 3. The Work of the Imagination – 4. Prose and Poetry – 5. The Human Voice – 6. Choral Singing – 7. How to Listen to Music – 8. The Magic Power of a Gesture – 9. Beauty – 10. Idealization as a Means of Creation – 11. A Living Masterpiece – 12. Building the Temple – Postface.

224 – THE POWERS OF THOUGHT

1. The Reality of Spiritual Work – 2. Thinking the Future – 3. Psychic Pollution – 4. Thoughts are Living Beings – 5. How Thought Produces Material Results – 6. Striking a Balance between Matter and Spirit – 7. The Strength of the Spirit – 8. Rules for Spiritual Work – 9. Thoughts as Weapons – 10. The Power of Concentration – 11. Meditation – 12. Creative Prayer – 13. Reaching for the Unattainable.

225 – HARMONY AND HEALTH

1. Life Comes First – 2. The World of Harmony – 3. Harmony and Health – 4. The Spiritual Foundations of Medicine – 5. Respiration and Nutrition – 6. Respiration: I. The Effects of Respiration on Health – II. How to Melt into the Harmony of the Cosmos – 7. Nutrition on the Different Planes – 8. How to Become Tireless – 9. Cultivate an Attitude of Contentment.

226 – THE BOOK OF DIVINE MAGIC

1. The Danger of the Current Revival of Magic – 2. The Magic Circle of the Aura – 3. The Magic Wand – 4. The Magic Word – 5. Talismans – 6. Is Thirteen an Unlucky Number – 7. The Moon – 8. Working with Nature Spirits – 9. Flowers and Perfumes – 10. We All Work Magic – 11. The Three Great Laws of Magic – 12. The Hand – 13. The Power of a Glance – 14. The Magical Power of Trust –

15. Love, the Only True Magic – 16. Never Look for Revenge – 17. The Exorcism and Consecration of Objects – 18. Protect Your Dwelling Place.

227 – GOLDEN RULES FOR EVERYDAY LIFE

1. Life: our most precious possession – 2. Let your material life be consistent with your spiritual life – 3. Dedicate your life to a sublime goal – 4. Our daily life: a matter that must be transformed by the spirit – 5. Nutrition as Yoga – 6. Respiration – 7. How to recuperate energy – 8. Love makes us tireless – 9. Technical progress frees man for spiritual work – 10. Furnishing your inner dwelling – 11. The outer world is a reflection of your inner world – 12. Make sure of a good future by the way you live today – 13. Live in the fullness of the present – 14. The importance of beginnings... etc.

228 – LOOKING INTO THE INVISIBLE
Intuition, Clairvoyance, Dreams

1. The Visible and the Invisible – 2. The Limited Vision of the Intellect, The Infinite Vision of Intuition – 3. The Entrance to the Invisible World : From Yesod to Tiphareth – 4. Clairvoyance : Activity and Receptivity – 5. Should We Consult Clairvoyants ? – 6. Love and Your Eyes Will be Opened – 7. Messages From Heaven – 8. Visible and Invisible Light: Svetlina and Videlina – 9. The Higher Degrees of Clairvoyance – 10. The Spiritual Eye – 11. To See God – 12. The True Magic Mirror: The Universal Soul – 13. Dream and Reality – 14. Sleep, an Image of Death – 15. Protect Yourself While You Are Asleep – 16. Astral Projection While Asleep – 17. Physical and Psychic Havens – 18. The Sources of Inspiration – 19. Sensation is Preferable to Vision.

229 – THE PATH OF SILENCE

1. Noise and Silence – 2. Achieving Inner Silence – 3. Leave Your Cares at the Door – 4. Make Your Meals an Exercise in Silence – 5. Silence, a Reservoir of Energies – 6. The Inhabitants of Silence – 7. Harmony, the Essential Condition for Inner Silence – 8. Silence, the Essential Condition for Thought – 9. The Quest for Silence is the Quest for the Centre – 10. Speech and the Logos – 11. A Master Speaks in Silence – 12. The Voice of Silence is the Voice of God – 13. The Revelations of a Starry Sky – 14. A Silent Room.

Editor-Distributor

Editions PROSVETA S.A. – B.P. 12 – 83601 Fréjus Cedex (France)

Distributors

AUSTRIA
MANDALA
Verlagsauslieferung für Esoterik
A-6094 Axams, Innsbruckstraße 7

BELGIUM
PROSVETA BENELUX
Van Putlei 105 B-2548 Lint
N.V. MAKLU Somersstraat 13-15
B-2000 Antwerpen
VANDER S.A.
Av. des Volontaires 321
B-1150 Bruxelles

BRAZIL
NOBEL SA
Rua da Balsa, 559
CEP 02910 - São Paulo, SP

BRITISH ISLES
PROSVETA
The Doves Nest
Duddleswell, Uckfield,
East Sussex TN22 3JJ

CANADA
PROSVETA Inc.
1565 Montée Masson
Duvernay est, Laval, Que. H7E 4P2

CYPRUS
THE SOLAR CIVILISATION BOOKSHOP
PO Box 4947
Nicosie

GERMANY
EDIS GmbH
Daimlerstr.5
D - 8029 Sauerlach

GREECE
PROFIM MARKETING Ltd
Ifitou 13
17563 P. Faliro
Athens

HOLLAND
STICHTING
PROSVETA NEDERLAND
Zeestraat 50
2042 LC Zandvoort

HONG KONG
HELIOS – J. Ryan
P.O. Box 8503
General Post Office, Hong Kong

IRELAND
PROSVETA IRL.
84 Irishtown – Clonmel

ITALY
PROSVETA Coop. a r.l.
Cas. post. 13046 – 20130 Milano

LUXEMBOURG
PROSVETA BENELUX
Van Putlei 105 B-2548 Lint

MEXICO
COLOFON S.A.
Pitagora 1143
Colonia del Valle
03 100 Mexico, D.F.

NORWAY
PROSVETA NORDEN
Postboks 5101
1501 Moss

PORTUGAL
PUBLICAÇÕES
EUROPA-AMERICA Ltd
Est Lisboa-Sintra KM 14
2726 Mem Martins Codex

SPAIN
ASOCIACIÓN PROSVETA ESPAÑOLA
C/ Ausias March n° 23 Ático
SP-08010 Barcelona

SWITZERLAND
PROSVETA
Société Coopérative
CH - 1808 Les Monts-de-Corsier

UNITED STATES
PROSVETA U.S.A.
P.O. Box 49614
Los Angeles, California 90049

VENEZUELA
J.P. Leroy
Apartado 51 745
Sabana Grande
1050 A – Caracas

PRINTED IN FRANCE IN JUNE 1991
EDITIONS PROSVETA, Z.I. DU CAPITOU
B.P.12 – 83601 FRÉJUS
FRANCE

– N° d'impression : 1927 –
Dépôt légal : June 1991
Printed in France